Hearts, butterflies, and buckles are the stock and trade of today's trendiest jewelers. But did you know that these jewelry motifs—from the heart earrings you bought as a teenager at Claire's to the pearl necklace you remember your grandmother wearing to the hair brooches popular at the Met Gala—take their cues from the Victorian era?

Hearts became trendy when Queen Victoria first began to wear them as part of her mourning wardrobe. Butterflies, an emblem for immortality, were all the rage in brooches. And buckles, representing protection and fidelity, were popularized as the symbol for the exclusive Victorian society the Order of the Garter.

Taking readers into the secret history of more than sixty symbols, motifs, and jewels, *Secret Language of Victorian Jewelry* is the first of its kind—a guide that marries the past and present, helping us to better understand our wardrobe choices and choose the most meaningful and intentional gifts.

Armed with this manual, jewelry enthusiasts will be able to decode the hidden significance behind family heirlooms and celebrity wardrobe choices alike. All jewelry makes a statement—*Secret Language of Victorian Jewelry* will empower you to choose yours.

Secret Language of Victorian Jewelry

SECRET LANGUAGE OF VICTORIAN JEWELRY

The History and Lore of Gems, Charms, and Talismans

Amy Azzarito

ILLUSTRATIONS BY BRIAN REEDY

CLARKSON POTTER/PUBLISHERS
NEW YORK

For Marilyn Azzarito,
for the hours spent peering
into your jewelry box.

And to Stella Fujiwara,
for the jewelry box hours yet to come.

Contents

BRACELET STACK,
CIRCA 1840.

Introduction

The jewelry we choose for ourselves silently communicates volumes about our personalities, beliefs, and unique stories. It is a visual language that has been documented by archeologists who uncovered shell beads dating back 135,000 years. These early humans weren't wearing jewelry to keep up with fashion trends; they believed their necklaces, earrings, and bracelets were imbued with supernatural powers—from ensuring a safe passage to the afterlife to warding off evil spirits in this one.

These pieces—known as amulets, but sometimes called talismans or charms—conferred special protections or abilities on the wearer based on something inherent in their design (i.e., the shape, material, or color). The word *amulet* is derived from the Latin term *amuletum,* which signifies a means of defense. Every culture has an amuletic tradition; it is part of our humanity. Magical thinking gives us control over our lives. That belief system is interwoven with the history of jewelry and is the basis for its communicative properties.

Similar to citizens of the ancient world, many people today still believe in a malignant force called the evil eye, the harbinger of ill health and poor fortune. The evil eye is believed to be summoned about by a malevolent glare from another person, usually when the recipient is unaware. It is hard to overstate how worrisome it was for our ancestors 5,000 years ago. Amulets offered the only known protection.

In ancient Egypt, nearly all jewelry had some magical significance. Sometimes an amulet's material was thought to protect the wearer, like those made from shells from the Red Sea. Or, the charm's form might represent something specific. For example, a fish—obviously a great swimmer—was worn to prevent drowning. A frog was worn to ensure fertility, because so many of them appeared annually when the Nile flooded. Nearly every Roman relied on amuletic protection. Those with deep pockets turned to gemstones, like the opals that Roman generals carried into battle.

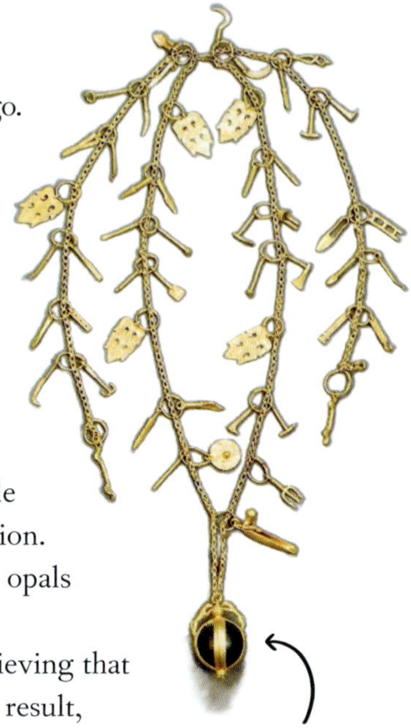

GOLD CHAIN WITH 52 AMULET-PENDANTS, A.D. 380–425.

Medieval people continued this line of thinking, believing that they lived in a world swarming with unseen spirits, so as a result, anxiety about these malevolent spirits drove much of their jewelry choices. The Church had a complicated relationship with amulets, historically condemning them as superstitious, a word that was used to denigrate anything deemed pagan. In practice, the pull of amuletic traditions was hard to shake, and early Christians adapted those pagan customs, often incorporating Christian symbols and text. The use of amuletic objects—particularly, precious stones and engraved gems—to combat negative forces in the world continued through the Enlightenment.

By the late nineteenth century, people began to refer to their talismans by the less superstitious name of *mascots*. Family members sending soldiers off to

CORAL NECKLACE WITH CHARMS THAT INCLUDE THOR'S HAMMER, A CROSS, THE HEWBREW LETTER *SHIN* AND A ROOSTER, 1870.

war (think the Napoleonic Wars in Europe) would often give their loved ones a tiny mascot to be tucked into a pocket in hopes of a safe return home. These trinkets were the predecessors of our lucky sports team mascots.

This was a time when nearly every aspect of behavior was governed by a strict set of rules and etiquette. In this world of repressed expression, symbolic meaning was everywhere. There was floriography, which uncovered the hidden meanings behind flowers; there was a secret language of stamps, where the placement of postage could convey a coded meaning; colors had symbolic meanings; and then there was jewelry.

Given its intimate nature, jewelry was particularly ripe for Victorian symbolism. There were motifs such as the heart or the anchor, which symbolized fidelity, hope, trust, or the arrow, which glitters but also wounds. The materials also held significance, as gemstones had been imbued with meaning since the days of the ancients. For example, amethyst combined with pearls could symbolize loss. Coral was for protection, and turquoise was for love and loyalty.

Consider this volume your code breaker as we journey back to a world where Queen Victoria ruled, the transatlantic cable had just been invented, and stagecoach was the way to travel. As we cover a wide range of sixty jewels and symbolic motifs, we'll learn about the amuletic traditions of each and the stunning jewelry they inspired.

Even though our modern fashion trends might move at the blink of an eye, jewelry has staying power. A pearl necklace worn by one's grandmother has a preciousness that few other objects possess. But it's the jewels we choose for ourselves—whether from a store or an estate sale—that will be our true personal legacy. So what will it be? A shooting star? A heart locket? Let's find out.

1950s CHARM BRACELET.

HENRY VIII'S (1491–1547) ONLY SURVIVING SON, PRINCE EDWARD (1537–1553), IN HIS ACORN-BUTTON COAT.

A C O R N

Meaning: THE JOURNEY OF TRANSFORMATION. FERTILITY AND GOOD FORTUNE.

Protective Power: BRINGS SAFETY AND GOOD LUCK.

A symbol of growth, patience, and transformation, the acorn is a powerful protective talisman, a lucky charm that conjures resilience: Acorns can survive harsh conditions and still grow into mighty oaks. It's because of this power to create an oak tree that the acorn is also used to represent the creation of life and fertility.

The House of Tudor, the iconic English fifteenth-century dynastic family, fully embraced acorn iconography. Henry VIII created a private emblem with his second wife, Anne Boleyn (mother to Queen Elizabeth I), that consisted of a honeysuckle, a symbol of love and devotion, and an acorn, in hopes that she would give birth to a son. In this case, the charm didn't seem to work—after all Henry infamously had Anne beheaded so he could continue his quest for an heir. When he finally did have a son, he reached again for the acorn motif, commissioning a portrait of Edward VI wearing a jacket fastened with acorn buttons to symbolize the continuation of Henry's royal lineage, from seed to great oak.

The acorn also holds significance in the modern British royal family. When Catherine Middleton married Prince William, she wore diamond acorn earrings, a gift from her parents designed to echo the Middleton family's coat of arms. The acorn is a nod to the Princess of Wales's childhood home, the aptly named Oak Acre in West Berkshire, England, which was surrounded by oak trees. The princess's collection includes other pieces of acorn jewelry, like a diamond oak leaf and pearl acorn brooch, as well as an acorn pendant charm, both from Asprey London.

ANCIENT ROMAN FUNERARY WREATH.

An acorn is a promise of big things!

ACORN HAIR PINS, CIRCA 1830.

A VICTORIAN CHARM FOR POTENTIAL AND PROSPERITY. COURTESY OF ERICA WEINER.

ANCIENT GREEK EARRING.

"Mighty oaks from little acorns grow."

—CHAUCER, FOURTEENTH CENTURY

ACORN & OAKS CHARM BRACELET. COURTESY OF MICHAEL MICHAUD.

THIS BROOCH SPELLS OUT "DEAREST" (DIAMOND, EMERALD, AMETHYST, RUBY, EMERALD, SAPPHIRE, TOURMALINE). COURTESY OF INEZ STODEL.

ACROSTIC

Meaning: EACH LETTER OF THE ALPHABET CORRESPONDS TO THE NAME OF A DIFFERENT PRECIOUS COLORED STONE.

Protective Power: A TOKEN OF REMEMBRANCE.

The concept of assigning a gemstone to each letter of the alphabet came from those masters of romance, the French. In 1806, Mellerio dits Meller, the French jewelry house who once outfitted Marie Antoinette, created an acrostic ring that spelled J'ADORE. *Ooh la la!* The elite took notice.

Always one to pay attention to fashion, Napoleon ordered acrostic pieces for his mother, sister, and Empress Joséphine to mark sentimental occasions. For Joséphine, Napoleon commissioned bracelets from his favorite jeweler, Marie-Étienne Nitot (who later founded the House of Chaumet), spelling out the names of "Eugène" and "Hortense"—Joséphine's two children.

Part of Napoleon's grand plan was for France to once again become a leader in the world of fashion. That was a little challenging when France was at war with its greatest fashion consumer, the British. But by 1815, the British had won the war, Napoleon had been exiled to Saint Helena, and the Victorians felt safe to once again adopt French fashion.

So in 1862, when Queen Victoria's oldest son, Albert Edward, the Prince of Wales, proposed to Princess Alexandra of Denmark, he chose something sentimental. He commissioned an acrostic ring from the London jewelers Garrard

& Co. The ring was set with **B**eryl; **E**merald; **R**uby; **T**opaz; **J**acinth (the *i* and *j* were considered interchangeable), a type of zircon; and **E**merald to spell out **Bertie,** his nickname. Bespoke, intimate, and only ever so slightly narcissistic.

SPELLS ELISABETH, CIRCA 1800.

For those Victorians who didn't have a royal jeweler on speed dial, popular sentiments expressed in acrostic rings were **"Regard," "Adore,"** or **"Dearest."** The concept spoke to the Victorian interest in wordplay. Were people really saying "regard" to each other? It's unclear, but **R**uby, **E**merald, **G**arnet, **A**methyst, **R**uby, and **D**iamond were easy-to-procure and popular gemstones. Jewelers often had to get creative using old gem names to get a necessary letter (such as calling garnet "vermeil" to get the letter V).

A handful of modern jewelry designers have revived the acrostic jewelry trend, which speaks to our fascination with personalization. The names of children, pets, dates, or even special places can also be spelled out in gemstones as a wearable secret.

WEDDING BELLS IN 1863 FOR PRINCE ALBERT (1841–1910) AND PRINCESS ALEXANDRA OF DENMARK (1844–1925).

THESE GEMTONE DROP EARRINGS SPELL OUT "LOVE YOU" COURTESY OF SCRIBE JEWELRY.

IN 1806, NAPOLEON BONAPARTE (1769–1821) ADOPTED HIS WIFE JOSÉPHINE'S (1763–1814) TWO CHILDREN, EUGÈNE AND HORTENSE. HE MARKED THE OCCASION WITH THE GIFT OF THESE TWO BRACELETS THAT SPELLED OUT EACH CHILD'S NAME IN GEMSTONES.

JEWELRY THAT SPELLS IT OUT.

GEMSTONE ALPHABET

A
Amethyst

B
Blue Topaz

C
Citrine

D
Diamond

E
Emerald

F
Feldspar

G
Garnet

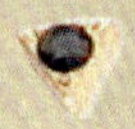
H
Hematite

I
Iolite

J
Jade

K
Kunzite

L
Lapis

M
Moonstone

N
Nacre (Pearl)

O
Opal

P
Peridot

Q
Quartz (Rose)

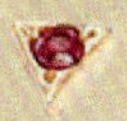
R
Ruby

S
Sapphire

T
Turquoise

U
Uvite

V
Verdelite

W
White Sapphire

X
Xonolite

Y
Yellow Sapphire

Z
Zircon (Blue)

JEWELER ERICA WEINER'S GEMSTONE ALPHABET AND ACROSTIC NECKLACES SPELLING "TAKEN" AND "DARLING." COURTESY OF ERICA WEINER JEWELRY.

THIS STONE WAS SAID TO BE A FAVORITE OF SAINT VALENTINE, WHO WORE AN AMETHYST RING ENGRAVED WITH THE IMAGE OF THE LOVE GOD, CUPID.

AMETHYST

Meaning: ROYALTY AND TEMPERANCE.

Protective Power: PROTECTS AGAINST BLACK MAGIC AND NEGATIVITY (AND ALSO FROM INTOXICATION).

Birthstone: FEBRUARY.

The fair maiden Amethyste was on her way to worship at the Temple of Diana when she attracted unwanted attention from Bacchus, the god of wine. As she fled from him, Bacchus became enraged by her refusal. Amethyste prayed to Diana (the protectress of women), who answered her pleas by turning the distressed damsel into a statue of pure white quartz. When Bacchus saw the lifeless Amethyste, he felt remorse and poured wine over her as a peace offering, turning the stone purple.

Believed by the ancient Greeks to prevent intoxication—after all, our maiden Amethyste certainly repels Bacchus—this is one of the few purple gemstones in existence. In the ancient world, the color purple was reserved for royalty due to the expense of producing even a single ounce of purple dye, so the amethyst was deemed regal by association.

Throughout the Middle Ages, the stone was believed to have powerful healing and protective capabilities. Many Crusaders attached amethyst beads to rosaries before embarking on their journeys. The gem was sacred to Tibetan Buddhists, who used it in prayer beads. It's also a significant stone in Judaism, where it represents the warrior tribe of Gad and was thought to inspire courage.

Large deposits of amethyst were found in Brazil in the nineteenth century, which caused its commercial value (and allure) to plummet. But for a stone that can ward off drunkenness, calm the mind, and assist in wise decisions, price may be irrelevant.

THE GEMSTONE WAS BELIEVED TO PREVENT NIGHTMARES AND INDUCE A PEACEFUL SLEEP AND HEALING DREAMS.

In the Egyptian Book of the Dead, heart-shaped amethysts are placed on the deceased's body as a symbol of wisdom in life.

CIRCA 1830.

ROMAN FIRST CENTURY A.D.

CIRCA 1830.

CIRCA 1830.

PRINCESS AUGUSTA (1768–1840), A DAUGHTER OF QUEEN CHARLOTTE AND GEORGE III (THE BRITISH KING WHO LOST THE U.S. COLONIES).

ANCHOR

Meaning: HOPE, STABILITY, AND STEADFASTNESS.

Protective Power: PROVIDES STABILITY AND SECURITY IN THE STORMY SEAS OF LIFE.

The anchor symbol was first devised by the Greeks in 400 B.C., and has been used throughout the world, for more than 2,400 years. It evokes sailors at sea, protecting their homeland and exploring the unknown. Used during harsh storms to provide stability, the symbol encompasses hope and steadfastness. It was adopted by early Christians as a reminder of a hope for the afterlife.

Princess Augusta, the sixth child of George III and Queen Charlotte, had an enamel anchor pendant that was a favorite accessory. Queen Charlotte kept such a close eye on her six daughters that the girls described their household as "the nunnery." The king preferred his daughters to his sons and was opposed to any suggestions that they marry and leave the royal nest. So when the royal family traveled to the seaside resort town of Weymouth in Dorset, it was a literal breath of fresh air to the sequestered royal princesses. Princess Augusta bathed in the sea, spent hours watching the ships from shore, and even took tours of naval vessels. She wore the anchor as both an emblem of that love of the sea and of her close relationship with her brother, William IV, known as the Sailor King.

The anchor still resonates as a symbol today. The luxury British jewelry brand Cece Jewellery has an anchor as one of their cornerstone motifs. It's meant to be worn during times of change and upheaval as a reminder to stay grounded.

SHARK & ANCHOR CHARM. COURTESY OF CECE JEWELLERY.

CIRCA 1970. COURTESY OF INEZ STODEL.

"We should not moor a ship with one anchor, or our life with one hope."

—EPICTETUS, THE PHILOSOPHER WHO DEVELOPED STOICISM

PRINCESS AUGUSTA, CIRCA 1802.

LATE NINETEENTH CENTURY. COURTESY OF INEZ STODEL.

NINETEENTH-CENTURY ANCHOR PATTERN.

THIS STYLE OF JEWELED HEADBAND IS KNOWN AS A FERRONIÈRE. FIRST WORN IN RENAISSANCE ITALY, IT WAS REVIVED IN THE EARLY NINETEENTH CENTURY.

AQUAMARINE

Meaning: SPIRITUAL LOVE, PEACE, COURAGE, AND JOY.

Protective Power: GUARDS THOSE AT SEA, IMPROVES MENTAL POWERS, AND FIGHTS PROCRASTINATION.

Birthstone: MARCH.

Some believe aquamarine was formed from the tears of sea nymphs, while others say it was the treasure of mermaids. Whether tears or treasure, there is no debating the stone's connection to the ocean. Its name derives from the Latin meaning "water of the sea."

In 1980, the world's largest cut aquamarine was unearthed in Brazil. The one-hundred-pound crystal was so heavy that the three prospectors who found it accidentally dropped the stone as they tried to haul it to the surface, shattering it into three pieces that turned out to be more manageable. The largest piece (about sixty pounds) was sent to Germany, where it was carved into a 10,000-plus carat obelisk and was donated to the Smithsonian Institution in 2011.

Leaving aside the world's *largest* aquamarine, perhaps the most *famous* one was the 13-carat emerald-cut stone set in yellow gold gifted to Princess Diana from her BFF Lucia Flecha de Lima—that's some friendship. The princess wore it on her left hand post-divorce, exchanging one blue stone (her sapphire engagement ring) for another. The ring is now in the collection of Meghan, Duchess of Sussex, who flashed it at her 2018 wedding to Prince Harry.

CIRCA 1950. COURTESY OF INEZ STODEL.

CIRCA 1920. COURTESY OF INEZ STODEL.

THE STONE IS SACRED TO APHRODITE, WHOSE NAME MEANS "BORN OF THE FOAM."

THE WORLD'S LARGEST AQUAMARINE.

CIRCA 1827.

CIRCA 1915. COURTESY OF INEZ STODEL.

"The lovely aquamarine, which seems to have come from some mermaid's treasure house. In the depths of a summer sea, has charms not to be denied."

—PLINY THE ELDER, CIRCA A.D. 50

GIVEN AS A ROMANTIC GIFT, IT MEANT "AN ARROW TO YOUR HEART."

ARROW

Meaning: LOVE, STRENGTH, COURAGE, AND RESILIENCE.

Protective Power: AS SPIRITUAL ARMOR, GIVES ONE THE BRAVERY NEEDED TO OVERCOME OBSTACLES.

It was during the time of Cleopatra that the mythological character of Cupid acquired his bow and arrow: Once shot, a person or deity was filled with uncontrollable desire. Cupid's arrow was a frequent motif in Medieval stories of courtly and romantic love.

The Victorians were extremely fond of history, and the arrow was the perfect marriage of their obsession with Medieval courtly love (just imagine knights wielding arrows on behalf of distressed damsels!) and their love of the mythological figure of Diana.

CIRCA 1890. COURTESY OF ERIE BASIN.

Hair ornaments known as Cupid's arrows or Cupid's darts were the must-have accessory of the nineteenth century. The arrow was made in two pieces and worn as if it had just grazed the head.

Diana, the Roman goddess of the hunt, moon, and nature was strong, quick, and clever. Her independence and free spirit made her a (proto) feminist role model. Arrow jewelry evoking Diana's power was extremely popular—and with a nod to Cupid? Even better.

NINETEENTH CENTURY. COURTESY OF INEZ STODEL.

In Japan, the arrow is a sacred symbol believed to bring good luck and ward off evil. At New Year's, the Japanese often buy a decorative arrow from Shinto shrines, known as a "demon-breaking arrow," to ward off misfortune in the coming year.

NINETEENTH-CENTURY JAPANESE ILLUSTRATION OF CEREMONIAL TOYS FOR THE NEW YEAR.

Bull's-eye: In 1825, a play about the story of Swiss folk hero William Tell, who famously shoots an apple off his son's head, premiered in London. It was a huge success and became a standard in Britain and America.

CIRCA 1970. COURTESY OF ERIE BASIN.

An arrow worn downward symbolized peace.

ARROW HAIR PIN, CIRCA 1831.

ANCIENT
GREEK BEE
PENDANT OF
TWO BEES
DROPPING
HONEY INTO
THEIR HIVE.

B E E

Meaning: WISDOM, HARD WORK, FERTILITY, AND PERSEVERANCE.

Protective Power: ATTRACTS WELL-BEING AND WEALTH.

The Egyptians believed that when the tears of the sun god Ra hit the ground, they were transformed into bees. To harness the insect's pollinating and honey-producing power, Egyptians placed hives on boats that floated down the Nile, taking advantage of the blooms along the riverbanks. In classical Greece (fifth and fourth centuries B.C.), the priestesses of the Great Goddess, the singular matriarchal deity, were known as *melissae* (bees). And in the Middle Ages, bees were a critical component of monastic gardens.

Reverence and appreciation of this honey-producing insect extended to jewelry. In 1653, the tomb of the fifth-century king Childeric I (ruler of the northern

Roman empire) was discovered to have been decorated with an awe-inspiring three hundred gold bees. Roman-obsessed Napoleon was so inspired that he adopted the bee as his symbol. To avoid confusion about who was in charge, he decreed that only those in his inner circle could wear the bee. Dukes could wear stars, but below a duke neither stars nor bees were acceptable.

The rules on bee-wearing relaxed by the late nineteenth century, when Tiffany & Co. created a line of gold, silver, and often bejeweled bee-themed "scatter pins" (so called because women liked to wear them scattered around their necklines). The Irish actor Andrew Scott wore a trio of Boucheron gold bees from 1948 similarly scattered around his neck at the 2024 Met Gala. Some things never change.

THE BEE WAS THE SYMBOL OF THE ANCIENT GREEK CITY OF EPHESOS AND REPRESENTED THE CITY'S AGRICULTURAL WEALTH.

BELLE ÉPOQUE BUMBLEBEE BROOCH, CIRCA 1900. COURTESY OF BELL AND BIRD.

LOCKET WITH ENAMELED BEE, CIRCA 1880. COURTESY OF INEZ STODEL.

CIRCA 1960. COURTESY OF ERIE BASIN.

A REMINDER TO SAVOR THE SWEETNESS OF LIFE BY THE BRITISH JEWELER CECE JEWELLERY.

"That which is not good for the beehive cannot be good for the bees."

—MARCUS AURELIUS

GOLD BEES OF THE FRANKISH RULER CHILDERIC I (DIED 481), A BARBARIAN ALLY OF THE ROMANS. THE BEES WERE DISCOVERED IN HIS TOMB IN 1653.

BYZANTINE
EARRING (SIXTH TO
SEVENTH CENTURY).

BLUE SAPPHIRE

Meaning: SYMBOL OF FRIENDSHIP AND FAITHFULNESS.

Protection: GUARDS AGAINST DECEIT AND TREACHEROUS PLOTS.

Birthstone: SEPTEMBER.

While sapphires naturally occur in virtually every color—blues to greens, yellows to oranges and even pinks and purples—it's the deep blue that is the most renowned (and expensive). It's a color that evokes the sky, and therefore the heavens, making this the gemstone of the divine. The Persians believed that the entire world rested on a giant sapphire, and the stone's reflection created blue skies. In ancient Rome, it was the stone of the god Jupiter and was often worn by soldiers to evoke his protection. Worn as beads, the gemstones were coveted not for their monetary value but for their talismanic properties.

FOURTEENTH CENTURY.

Medieval philosophers ascribed magical and spiritual attributes to all gemstones, but they particularly loved the sapphire, which had such a long list of powers that it was the most desired stone of the period. According to these wisemen, it was an antidote to poison, and could prevent fevers and promote general health. It protected the wearer from fraud, conquered envy, and averted terror. It was also believed that contemplating the deep blue of the sapphire would raise men's souls to a heavenly level; the gemstone had the power to make the wearer beloved by both God and man.

Something old
Something new
Something borrowed
Something blue,
and a [silver]
sixpence in her shoe.

In 1840, on the eve of their wedding, Prince Albert gave his future bride, Queen Victoria, a sapphire brooch with the 20- to 30-carat blue stone surrounded by twelve diamonds. The twenty-year-old queen was so enamored of the brooch that she wore it on her wedding day. It is quite likely that her sapphire started the wedding trend of wearing "something blue." Victoria designated the jewel "a royal heirloom belonging to the crown." It has since been worn by every queen or consort in the British royal family.

In 1981, when choosing her engagement ring, another twenty-year-old bride, the young Diana Spencer, was immediately drawn to a 12-carat Ceylon sapphire ring set inside a diamond halo. She later said that it reminded her of her mother's wedding ring. In truth the ring's designer, Garrards, had been directly inspired by Queen Victoria's wedding day brooch. It was a fact perhaps unknown to Diana, who received a lot of criticism from the British press for choosing a ring from a jeweler rather than a royal heirloom.

IN THE BIBLE, GOD'S THRONE IS MADE OF SAPPHIRE. THE ROMANS AND EGYPTIANS BELIEVED IT TO BE THE STONE OF TRUTH AND JUSTICE.

CIRCA 1830s.

A MEDIEVAL RING (LATE THIRTEENTH TO FOURTEENTH CENTURY), KNOWN AS A STIRRUP RING, NAMED FOR ITS RESEMBLANCE TO EQUINE EQUIPMENT.

TWENTY-YEAR-OLD QUEEN VICTORIA (1819–1901) ON HER WEDDING DAY, WEARING HER SAPPHIRE PINNED TO HER CHEST.

The name "sapphire" comes from the Sanskrit words Sani (Saturn) and Priyah (precious).

A SÉVIGNÉ IS A FLAT SYMMETRICAL RIBBON BOW THAT WAS WORN LOW ON THE BODICE AND EVOLVED INTO A MORE ELABORATE JEWELED BOW.

B O W

Meaning: Love, romance, and connection.

Protective Power: Ties people together.

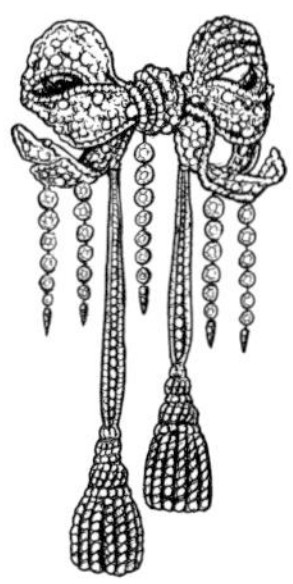

It was in the over-the-top French royal court of Louis XIV that simple fastening became elevated to luxury status. Ribbons were an equal-opportunity accessory—worn by men, women, and the king, who wanted to revive the French ribbon industry through his own trend-setting. The one-upmanship of the court meant that it wasn't long until the bows were made of jewels instead of ribbons.

It wasn't just the French who loved a jeweled bow: Later, in England, Queen Mary of Teck (great-grandmother to King Charles III) was so obsessed with the shape that she had six large diamond bow brooches in her collection. In her defense, some of them were gifts and some she had inherited from Queen Victoria—but she did also treat herself. The largest bow brooch in her collection, known as the Lover's Knot Brooch, was purchased from the London jeweler Garrard in 1932. While all the bow brooches from Mary's collection were worn frequently by Queen Elizabeth, she chose the Lover's Knot to wear to the wedding of Prince William and Catherine Middleton. Although Queen Mary had a Lover's Knot tiara that Princess Catherine has worn and is part of the same collection, none of the bow brooches have made a royal appearance since Queen Elizabeth II's death in 2022.

CIRCA 1940.
COURTESY OF
ERIE BASIN.

NINETEENTH
CENTURY.

Bows first appeared in jewelry in the glamorous seventeenth century French court of Louis XIV.

GILT WOOD RIBBON.
EIGHTEENTH CENTURY.

ALL EARRINGS WERE ONCE HOOP EARRINGS—AND EMBELLISHMENTS (PEARLS OR OTHER GEMS) WERE TIED ON WITH A BOW.

EIGHTEENTH CENTURY.

EIGHTEENTH CENTURY.

A BIG BUCKLE WAS DE RIGUEUR FOR 1830s FASHION.

B U C K L E

Meaning: LOYALTY, FIDELITY, AND PROTECTION.

Protective Powers: BINDS LOVE.

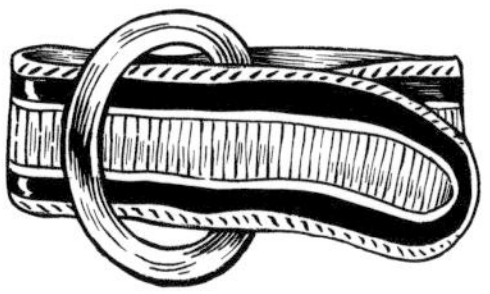

In 1348, the British king Edward III was dancing with his future daughter-in-law Joan, Countess of Salisbury, when to her embarrassment, one of her garters (bands used to hold up stockings) slipped off her leg. This was the fourteenth-century equivalent to having your underpants fall down. To quell the giggles, the king picked up the garter, placed it on his own leg, and said, "Shame on he who thinks evil of it."

The phrase became the motto of his new chivalric order: Knights of the Garter. He had been looking for a way to cement power and position, and an ultra-exclusive club (with a Knights of the Round Table vibe) seemed like the perfect way to do it. Spoiler alert: He was right, and it still exists today.

Waiting for the buckle connection? A medieval garter was often a piece of leather or cloth fastened with a **buckle**. At the time, both men and women wore stockings. And since this was well before the days of elastic, both men and women wore garters. (At the Order of the Garter initiation ceremony, a garter is placed on the leg of incoming knights, and on the left arm of new ladies.) Membership was (and still is) limited to twenty-four: twelve knight companions for the king and twelve for the Prince of Wales. Every June, they gather at Windsor Castle to celebrate Garter Day.

MEDIEVAL RING WITH BUCKLE, SEVENTEENTH CENTURY.

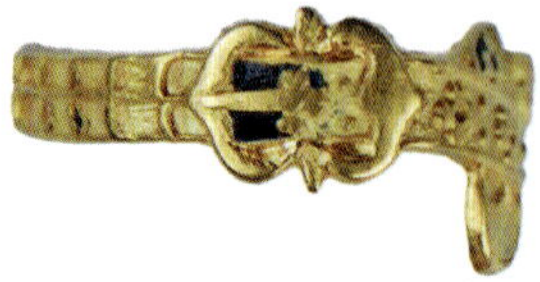

Victorians were enamored of the concept of medieval chivalry. The Order of the Garter fit the bill perfectly and the garter/buckle motif became a widespread reminder of what chivalry entailed: loyalty, fidelity, and protection. Soon, a nineteenth-century woman's outfit wasn't complete without a buckle at her waist (extra points if her other jewelry had buckles to match). When Queen Victoria wore a buckle ring to symbolize her membership in the Order of the Garter, her subjects took notice. Almost overnight, buckle jewelry became a fad throughout Europe, and buckles have been a thing ever since. Throughout the twentieth century and into the twenty-first, it has remained a jewelry staple, styled to fit the prevailing fashion.

ROYAL ORDER OF THE GARTER.

The circular shape of the belt and buckle evoked infinity, which, when gifted, represented a binding love.

BUCKLE BRACELET WORN AS PART OF MOURNING ATTIRE.

THE ANCESTOR OF BUCKLE JEWELRY (AND THE CRINGEY WEDDING TRADITION).

NINETEENTH CENTURY. COURTESY OF ERIE BASIN.

QUEEN LILI'UOKALANI OF HAWAII (1838–1917). IN 1887 SHE TRAVELED TO THE UK FOR QUEEN VICTORIA'S GOLDEN JUBILEE CELEBRATION TO REPRESENT HAWAII. ON HER TRIP, SHE PURCHASED THE BUTTERFLY BROOCH, WHICH IS WORN HERE IN HER HAIR.

BUTTERFLY

Meaning: TRANSFORMATION, BEAUTY, AND CREATIVITY.

Protective Power: SYMBOLIZING THE SOUL, THE BUTTERFLY IS A SIGN OF IMMORTALITY.

For more than eight thousand years, human cultures have seen the butterfly as a sign of the return (or presence) of a departed spirit. Aristotle called the butterfly a *psyche*, ancient Greek for "soul," inspired by the butterfly's final emergence from its chrysalis. In the ancient story of Cupid and Psyche, Psyche is granted immortality by Cupid's mother, Venus, and is often depicted with butterfly wings.

During the Victorian era, interest in natural history exploded. The average Victorian was obsessed with collecting and categorizing the natural world. Butterfly collecting became a popular hobby—particularly for the wealthy, who spared no expense to add the most rare and exotic varieties to their collections.

CIRCA 1890–1910.

The butterfly-collecting craze was also reflected in butterfly jewelry. The higher-end versions were made entirely of diamonds. Jewelers even added tiny springs behind the wings so the butterfly would appear to flutter when the wearer moved.

The metamorphosis of a caterpillar into a butterfly also connects the insect to new beginnings, creativity, and often to liberation. In the 1820s the butterfly became the emblem of the American women's suffrage movement—activists were known as Iron Butterflies.

CIRCA 1900. COURTESY OF ERIE BASIN.

A PORTRAIT OF A FAIRY, 1869.

BUTTERFLY BROOCH, CIRCA 1960. COURTESY OF ERIE BASIN.

ANCIENT GREEK (LATE SECOND TO FIRST CENTURY B.C.).

MARIE PÜTTLINGEN, COUNTESS OF KRIECHINGEN, 1832.

MONO NO AWARE
物の哀れ

A Japanese philosophical concert of impermanence where the fleeting beauty of the butterfly is a poignant reminder of the transient nature of life. This deeply resonated with Victorian sentimentalism.

THE INSPIRATION FOR PRINCESS LEIA'S BUNS, THE HOPI BUTTERFLY HAIRSTYLE INDICATES A LADY'S SINGLE STATUS.

IMAGE OF HERCULES,
LATE EIGHTEENTH
CENTURY.

CAMEO

Meaning: POWER, WEALTH, STATUS, AND DEVOTION TO THE GOD OR POLITICAL ENTITY DEPICTED.

Protective Power: THE POWER OF THE IMAGE IS CARRIED BY THE WEARER.

From Roman togas to Victorian ball gowns, cameos have been a popular adornment for thousands of years. These miniature, wearable sculptures are part of a stone-carving tradition that dates to the prehistoric Neolithic era. Carved from semi-precious stones, cameos were coveted symbols of wealth in ancient Greece and Rome. They often depicted gods or goddesses and were worn to publicly display an individual's association with a divine power.

During the Renaissance, all things ancient were *en vogue*—and that certainly included cameos. Passionate cameo collectors (like the Medici family) sparked a renewed interest in and revival of the art form. But the Renaissance cameo revival was nothing compared to the cameo frenzy of the eighteenth century after the discovery of the archaeological sites at Herculaneum and Pompeii.

Eighteenth-century tourists on the Grand Tour—that "edifying" two-to-three-year jaunt around Europe enjoyed by nearly all well-to-do young Britons—

loved to souvenir shop (see the British Museum), and cameos were favorite keepsakes. Depending on the budget, one could purchase antique cameos or cheaper, newly made "lava cameos" carved from the volcanic breccia that had preserved the archaeological sites for centuries.

THIS CAMEO IMAGE WAS TAKEN FROM BOTTICELLI'S FIFTEENTH-CENTURY PAINTING, THREE GRACES. IT CONVEYS, AT A SINGLE GLANCE, THAT THE WEARER KNOWS AND APPRECIATES ART.

On his military campaigns across Italy, Napoleon became enchanted by cameos (particularly ones with his own image). Not only did he bring ancient cameos back to France, but he also brought back talented cameo carvers whom he had abducted in Sicily. He founded a school in Paris to teach the art of cameo carving, staffing it with those purloined Sicilians. Both Napoleon and the Empress Joséphine had cameo crowns; Joséphine's is now in the collection of the Swedish royal family and is still used as the royal bridal tiara.

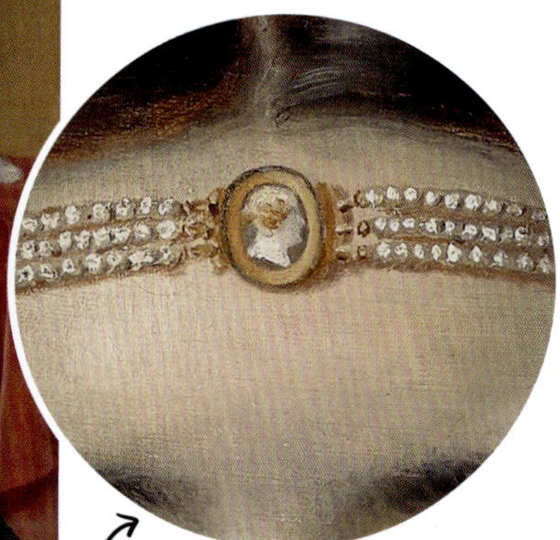

SOPHIE FREMIET (1797–1867), READY FOR AN EVENING AT THE THEATER, WAS ALSO A SUCCESSFUL NINETEENTH-CENTURY ARTIST.

MID-NINETEENTH CENTURY.

BRITISH CHAPS ON THE GRAND TOUR.

The origin of the phrase "a cameo appearance," a brief appearance of a star in a movie, can be traced back to this technique of carving gemstones.

THE MORE THE MERRIER. COUNT THE CAMEOS ON THIS NINETEENTH-CENTURY PRINCESS.

SIXTEENTH-
CENTURY KITTY
CUDDLE.

C A T

Meaning: GOOD FORTUNE AND PROSPERITY.

Protective Power: GUARDS AGAINST EVIL SPIRITS AND NEGATIVE ENERGY.

Many ancient societies, including the Greeks, Romans, Chinese, and Indians, revered the cat. One Thai tradition demanded the king be buried with his pet cats, who were provided with escape holes; when they found their way out, it signified that the royal soul had reached heaven. The early Chinese believed that one could tell the time of day by looking into the eyes of a cat. However, no one matched the ancient Egyptians for their fervent veneration of house cats. Those pampered pets were often just as bejeweled as their owners, dining on sacred fish from the Nile while wearing earrings, necklaces, and even nose rings.

In tenth-century Japan, cats were considered to be so valuable that only the nobility could afford to own one. A famous Japanese folktale tells of a cat that saved a feudal lord from a lightning strike by beckoning to him. Today, businesses and homeowners pay homage to that cat, known as Maneki Neko, the Fortune Cat, by placing him at the entrance of homes or shops, where he waves a single paw, for good luck and prosperity.

In Britain, unlike many other European countries, black cats were considered to be primarily lucky charms. In the nineteenth century, small glass black cats were placed in Christmas crackers (the popping party favor, not the snack food). They were intended to be carried in one's pocket or worn as a pendant to ensure good fortune.

MAGDALEINE PINCELOUP DE LA GRANGE (EIGHTEENTH CENTURY) WEARING A NECKLACE THAT ECHOES HER CAT'S COLLAR.

EGYPTIAN CUFF BRACELET.

NINETEENTH CENTURY. COURTESY OF ERIE BASIN.

A 1900S STICK PIN, TO HOLD THE TIE OF A CAT-OBSESSED GENTLEMAN.

ANCIENT EGYPTIAN RING DEPICTING A CAT WITH HER KITTENS THOUGHT TO SYMBOLIZE THE MYTH OF THE "FARAWAY GODDESS," IN WHICH A DEITY MUST BE COAXED BACK TO RETURNING TO THE NILE VALLEY AFTER HER DEPARTURE BRINGS CHAOS.

The Egyptian cat goddess Bastet was the protector of domestic life and goddess of fertility and childbirth.

JEWELRY-WEARING EGYPTIAN CAT STATUE REPRESENTING THE GODDESS BASTET.

EGYPTIAN RING WITH FELINE HEAD.

ROMAN CITRINE ENGRAVED WITH THE IMAGE OF BONUS EVENTUS (DIVINE PERSONIFICATION OF SUCCESS). "MONEY STONE" + DIETY = POWERFUL AMULET FOR SUCCESS.

CITRINE

Meaning: THE HAPPY STONE. ATTRACTS AND MAINTAINS WEALTH.

Protective Power: PROTECTS AGAINST ANGER, NEGATIVE ENERGY, AND DISEASE.

Birthstone: NOVEMBER (WITH TOPAZ).

A type of naturally occurring quartz, citrine is a newish gemstone, in that it was unknown to the Egyptians. It was, however, used by the ancient Greeks and Romans (so not *that* new). The stone is less valuable than its doppelgänger, topaz, and is often mistaken as such. Considering it's nearly impossible to discern the difference between the two with the naked eye, the misrepresentation isn't always nefarious. For those who wound up with citrine, there was an advantage; citrine is harder and wears better than its more expensive cousin.

The name *citrine* comes from the French word for "lemon." However, in ancient Greece, it was called a *chrysolitus*, which translates to "gold stone," and was thought to bring success (and money). In Scotland, where there are natural deposits of a uniquely dark, smoky citrine, it was used as an amulet by medieval Celts and Scots to protect against both physical ailments (the plague) and psychological ones (evil thoughts).

When Queen Victoria and Prince Albert acquired Balmoral Castle Estate in 1852, they threw themselves into the Scottish theme. Plaid was everywhere, even on the queen, who often wore tartan while in residence (a trend continued by the royal family today). Native Scottish citrine was used for kilt pins and shoulder brooches, and even on the handles of daggers and swords. The land once mined for citrine is now protected as Cairngorms National Park, which has made the Scottish stones from the Victorian era even more valuable.

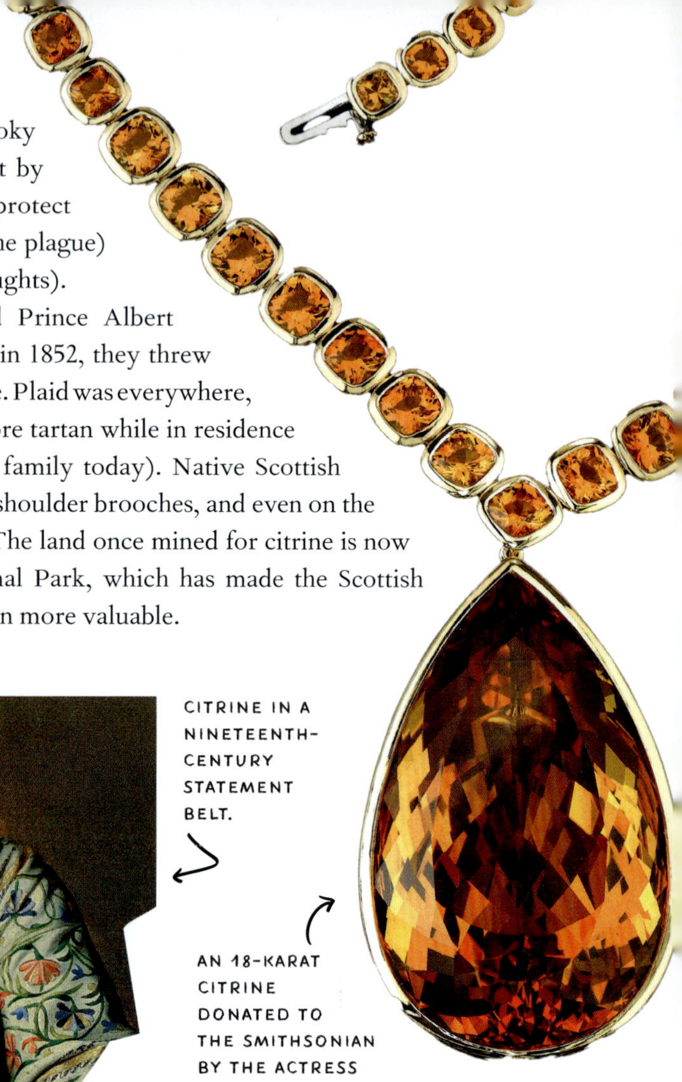

CITRINE IN A NINETEENTH-CENTURY STATEMENT BELT.

AN 18-KARAT CITRINE DONATED TO THE SMITHSONIAN BY THE ACTRESS ANGELINA JOLIE IN 2015.

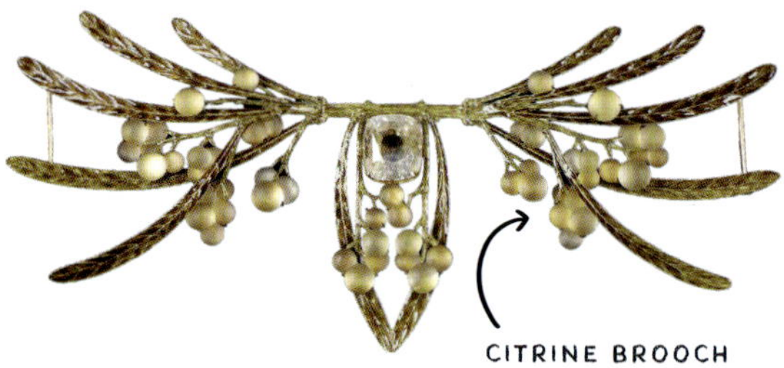

CITRINE BROOCH BY THE FRENCH ART NOUVEAU ARTIST RENÉ LALIQUE, CIRCA 1903.

NINETEENTH-
CENTURY
CITRINE
FERRONIÈRE.

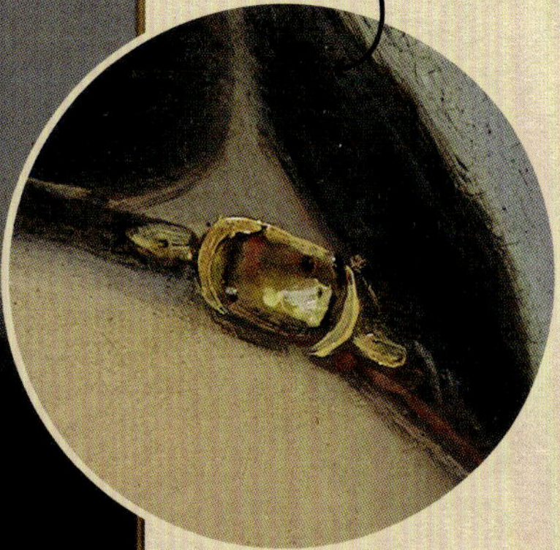

"She would take a citrine and make it look as important as a canary diamond."

—PROCLAIMED LEGENDARY VOGUE ACCESSORIES EDITOR CANDY PRATTS PRICE, DESCRIBING THE JEWELRY OF PALOMA PICASSO, WHO WAS PHOTOGRAPHED IN 1985 BY HORST P. HORST, WEARING THE LARGE CITRINE NECKLACE SHE HAD DESIGNED FOR TIFFANY AND CO.

1930S
SCANDINAVIAN
ART DECO.
COURTESY OF
ERIE BASIN.

EMPRESS EUGÉNIE (1826–1920) WEARING THE CLOVER FROM NAPOLEON III (1808–1873) PINNED TO THE BODICE OF HER DRESS.

CLOVER

Meaning: GOOD FORTUNE.

Protective Power: REPELS BAD LUCK.

According to Napoleonic lore, Emperor Bonaparte escaped an assassination attempt because he bent down to pick up a four-leaf clover. Although likely apocryphal, the story fueled the belief in the protective power of the charm.

When Louis-Napoleon Bonaparte (nephew of our lucky emperor) first met the Spanish countess Eugénie de Montijo, he was immediately captivated and set out to woo her. While strolling through the grounds of his home at Palais de Compiègne during the early days of their courtship, Eugénie marveled at how beautiful the dew looked on the early-morning grass: "Just like jewels." To commemorate the moment, Napoleon III commissioned a green enamel clover leaf brooch set with diamonds. Eugénie was charmed and the couple announced their engagement shortly after. Though her jewelry collection expanded as empress (crown jewels!), she frequently wore the sentimental clover, and it became something of a good-luck talisman for her.

Jacques Arpels, nephew of the Van Cleef & Arpels founder Estelle Arpels, collected four-leaf clovers and would give them to employees. The company had a history of making good-luck charms, even clover pendants. In 1968, the luxury jewelry house debuted a long necklace of clovers stylized to resemble the quatrefoil motif found in the Alhambra Palace in Granada, Spain. It was casual jewelry, perfect for the free-spirited 1960s, and was an immediate sensation, worn by celebrities like Grace Kelly and Elizabeth Taylor. Today it's a favorite of both Queen Camilla and Catherine, Princess of Wales.

NINETEENTH CENTURY. COURTESY OF ERIE BASIN.

A 1950s GOOD-LUCK CHARM FROM VAN CLEEF & ARPELS ("I WILL BRING YOU LUCK"). "TO BE LUCKY, YOU MUST BELIEVE IN LUCK." —JACQUES ARPELS. COURTESY OF INEZ STODEL.

ILLUSTRATION FOR A CIGARETTE CARD (SMALL COLLECTIBLE CARDS THAT WERE TUCKED INTO PACKS), 1889.

AMERICAN-MADE LUCKY CLOVER BROOCH, CIRCA 1900. COURTESY OF INEZ STODEL.

SHAMROCK VERSUS CLOVER

Shamrocks = always three leaves

Clovers = three or four leaves

NECKLACE WITH CLOVER LINKS, CIRCA 1880. COURTESY OF ERIE BASIN.

CLOVER BROOCH, 1900S. COURTESY OF ERIE BASIN.

BIA DE' MEDICI (1536–1542), DAUGHTER OF COSIMO I DE' MEDICI (1519–1574), WEARING HER FATHER'S ROMAN-STYLED MEDAL.

COINS

Meaning: LUCK, WEALTH, AND PROSPERITY.

Protective Power: WARDS OFF BAD LUCK OR PROTECTS FROM HARM.

Coins have been made into jewelry for thousands of years, worn by all social strata throughout the world. Jewelry has always represented wealth, and using coins certainly made for easy asset calculation. In ancient China, copper coins were minted with square holes through their centers. Called "cash coins," they were stacked in units of one hundred, three hundred, and one thousand and transported via strings rather than in pockets or purses.

The excitement around wearing ancient coins was a Renaissance revelation. After all, the entire Renaissance was inspired by the excavations at ancient Roman sites like Nero's Golden House, where ancient Roman coins were extremely plentiful. These tiny tangible relics of the ancient world were just as irresistible to the Renaissance consumer as they are to the modern one today. These coins have seen plagues, famine, despotic leaders and benevolent ones.

Powerful Renaissance families styled themselves on ancient Roman emperors and even created their own "coins" with Roman-style images. Cosimo I de' Medici, the Renaissance duke of Florence, had a portrait painted of his young

daughter after her death with a Roman-style medal around her neck to emphasize their father-daughter bond.

ROMAN NECKLACE FEATURING IMPERIAL PORTRAIT COINS OF EMPERORS AND EMPRESSES.

During the nineteenth century, coin jewelry became the ultimate souvenir for those lucky enough to visit the ancient sites. English jewelers stockpiled ancient coins via auctions and then spent several years churning out coin jewelry. This made it possible for those without a travel budget to look well traveled with a short jaunt to a local shop.

In the 1960s, the Italian luxury jewelry firm Bvlgari resurrected the ancient coin jewelry vibe with their Monete collection. Nicola Bulgari, grandson of the founder, had a personal passion for collecting antique coins and dreamt up this jewelry line with antique coins as the stars.

A team of specialists scoured international markets for rare, ancient coins to serve as "gems" for these Bvlgari creations. It was the era of La Dolce Vita (literally: the Fellini movie came out in 1960) and every '60s screen siren from Elizabeth Taylor to Sophia Loren to Grace Kelly was pictured with a piece of the Monete collection. The collection remains a celebrity favorite, still worn by the likes of Anne Hathaway, Taylor Swift, Adele, and Bella Hadid.

SEVENTEENTH-CENTURY MUGHAL COIN WITH THE SIGN OF PISCES, INDICATING THE MONTH OF ISSUE.

PAINTED BY POLISH ARTIST PANTALEON SZYNDLER, 1881.

ANCIENT GREEK COIN DEPICTING THE QUEEN CONSORT ARSINOË II.

See a penny, pick it up, all day long you'll have good luck.

A ROMAN BELT STAMPED TO INDICATE THAT IT IS MADE WITH "PURE GOLD" OF CONSTANTINOPLE.

MARGUERITE STERN (1866–1956) MARRIED INTO THE STERN FAMILY BANKING DYNASTY. SHE WAS A JEWISH ART COLLECTOR, WHOSE PROPERTY WAS SEIZED BY THE NAZIS DURING THE PARIS OCCUPATION.

CRESCENT MOON

Meaning: LOVE AND FERTILITY.

Protective Power: GUARDS AGAINST NEGATIVITY. CAN LEAD UNMARRIED PEOPLE TO FIND THEIR SOULMATES.

The *lunula*, "little moon" in Latin, was worn in the ancient world by women, children, and even beloved animals to evoke the protective powers of the Greek goddess Artemis (aka Diana), goddess of hunting and nature, who used the moon to her advantage. In the late sixteenth century, Queen Elizabeth I embraced the crescent moon because of its association with Diana, a virgin huntress and one of the few goddesses immune to love. The queen reinforced her purity and virtue by wearing crescent-shaped jewels in her portraits.

By the Victorian era, the crescent moon's association with moon goddesses gave the symbol an air of female empowerment and evoked the passing of seasons in one's life. Also tied to the menstrual cycle, these amulets were worn to protect women's health and fertility. Brides often wore brooches with crescent moon and flowers, known as honeymoon brooches, to represent the magic of the moon and the sweetness of flowers.

THIRTY-FIVE-YEAR-OLD CORINNA SALMON WAS THE DAUGHTER OF A PROMINENT ITALIAN BANKER. CIRCA 1893.

The moon can be used to represent different stages of a relationship. The crescent symbolizes the courtship period, while a full moon represents marriage.

NINETEENTH-CENTURY TIARA.

MARY II, QUEEN OF ENGLAND (1662–1694).

NINETEENTH CENTURY.

ROMAN, FIRST TO THIRD CENTURY.

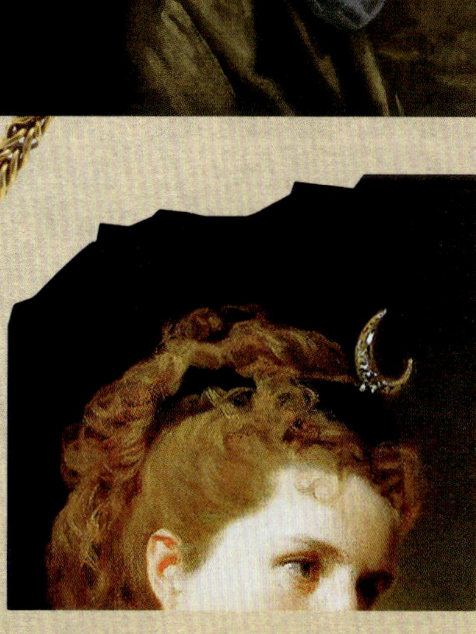

MATILDE DE AGUILERA Y GAMBOA, LADY OF FONTAGUD (1846–1874), DRESSED FOR A BALL.

CROSS MOTIFS HAVE BEEN USED IN NATIVE JEWELRY SINCE ANCIENT TIMES, PREDATING THE COMING OF CHRISTIANITY. THEY MIGHT HAVE SIGNIFIED THE SUN, STARS, OR THE FOUR DIRECTIONS: THEY ALSO MAY HAVE HAD A MEANING THAT HAS BEEN LOST. PORTRAIT, CIRCA NINETEENTH CENTURY.

CROSS

Meaning: WORN AS AN EXPRESSION OF FAITH AND DEVOTION.

Protective Power: SYMBOLIZING SACRIFICE, FAITH, AND VICTORY OVER DEATH.

The first cross was the ankh, an ancient Egyptian hieroglyph used to write "live," "alive," or "life." It was the Coptic Christians of Egypt in the fourth century who adopted it as a symbol of Christ's promise of everlasting life (early Roman Christians adopted the fertility symbol of the fish as a sign of their faith). When Emperor Constantine's mother claimed she had discovered the True Cross in 326 (the one used in the crucifixion), he proclaimed it as the public symbol of Christianity.

In 1683 Denmark, provost Christian Blichfeld started shifting some graves around St. Bendt's Church to make room for his wife's tomb—a little ghoulish, albeit romantic. In the process, he removed two royal tombs and discovered a Byzantine reliquary cross presumed to have belonged to Queen Dagmar, who had died four hundred years earlier in 1212. The relic, known as the Dagmar Cross, became a Danish national symbol.

So, in 1863, when King Frederick VII of Denmark's daughter, Alexandra, wed the Prince of Wales, it seemed only fitting that he gift her a copy of this ancient cross to take with her to England. But museum shop item this was not. King Frederick VII included a piece of silk from the grave of King Canute (eleventh-century ruler of England, Denmark, and Norway) and a sliver of wood said to be from the True Cross inside the reliquary. Alexandra (who was not understated when it came to jewelry) went a step further and sent the pendant to the Danish court jeweler, Julius Dideriksen, who mounted it onto a necklace made from 118 pearls and 2,000 diamonds. He even included two giant pearls that had been exhibited at the Great Exhibition at the Crystal Palace in 1851.

MADE BY THE AMERICAN ARTS AND CRAFTS JEWELER JOSEPHINE HARTWELL SHAW (1865–1941).

LATIN CROSS, OR *CRUX IMMISSA,* IS THE RECOGNIZABLE SYMBOL OF CHRISTIANITY. CIRCA NINETEENTH CENTURY.

Queen Alexandra wore the necklace and cross at her coronation in 1902, which caused such a demand for similar crosses that jewelers couldn't keep up. The cross remains such a potent symbol of Denmark that replicas—minus the two thousand diamonds, of course—are still given to Danish girls in connection with their baptisms or confirmations.

ELEVENTH-CENTURY CROSS THOUGHT TO BELONG TO QUEEN DAGMAR (1186–1212), KNOWN AS THE IDEAL CHRISTIAN QUEEN.

NINETEENTH CENTURY.

THE MALTESE CROSS'S EIGHT POINTS SYMBOLIZE THE EIGHT VIRTUES THAT A MEMBER OF THE ORDER OF ST. JOHN ACCEPTS, INCLUDING LOYALTY, PIETY, AND HONESTY.

USED AS A HIEROGLYPH TO WRITE THE WORDS *LIVE, ALIVE,* OR *LIFE.*

Queen Victoria was known to say that the cross was "an emblem of what [she had] to bear day after day" in reference to her long widowhood.

IF YOU SLEEP WITH A DAISY UNDER YOUR PILLOW, YOU WILL SUMMON YOUR WAYWARD LOVER HOME.

DAISY

Meaning: LOVE, INNOCENCE, AND MODESTY.

Protective Power: DAISY CHAINS ON A ROOF OR HANGING FROM A DOOR COULD PROTECT THE HOUSE FROM LIGHTNING. WEARING A DAISY CHAIN PROTECTS CHILDREN FROM BEING ABDUCTED BY FAIRIES.

The word *daisy* comes from an Old English word meaning "day's eye," because the flower opens in the morning and sleeps at night. In the Middle Ages, it was known as the flower of love. Knights wore these blooms in tournaments while ladies wore daisy crowns in their hair.

In French, the word for daisy is *marguerite* and it derives from the Greek word for "pearl." The English equivalent is Margaret, and the flower became an emblem of the many medieval English Margarets, French Marguerites, and Scandinavian Margrethes.

The daisy also happens to be the national flower of Denmark. Fittingly, King Frederik IX and Queen Ingrid of Denmark christened their firstborn Margrethe. The young crown princess was born just a week after the Nazis invaded the country in 1940, and her birth and namesake flower were seen as a positive omen. To celebrate, the Danish silversmith Georg Jensen designed a daisy jewelry collection as tribute. It became immediately popular, out of respect for the new princess but also as a symbol of national pride and Nazi resistance. Queen Margrethe II reigned as Queen of Denmark from January 14, 1972, until her abdication on January 14, 2024. The daisy became her signature, and she often wore the enamel jewelry created in her honor.

ANCIENT EGYPTIAN DAISY BEAD, CIRCA 1390–1352 B.C.

LOVE DIVINATION; *HE LOVES ME, HE LOVES ME NOT . . .*

THIS SMALL DAISY BROOCH WAS MADE TO HONOR ANOTHER ROYAL, PRINCESS MARGRIET OF THE NETHERLANDS, CIRCA 1945.

NO FLOWER? TRY SPINNING A GOLD DAISY ON A NECKLACE. WHEREVER THE DIAMOND LANDS WILL TELL YOU HOW MUCH LOVE THERE IS; LOVES ME – LITTLE / MUCH / MADLY / NOT AT ALL, CIRCA 1970. COURTESY OF INEZ STODEL.

DELICATE DAISY BROOCH AND EARRINGS, 1826.

A dream of daisies in the spring = good luck

A dream of daisies in the winter = bad luck

DANTE GABRIEL ROSSETTI'S (1828–1882) FAVORITE MUSE (AND ALSO MISTRESS), FANNY CORNFORTH (1835–1909), DEPICTED AS ROSAMUND CLIFFORD, A MEDIEVAL ENGLISH NOBLEWOMAN AND MISTRESS OF HENRY II.

LOCKET WITH EMBOSSED DAISY, CIRCA 1900. COURTESY OF ERIE BASIN.

CUPID'S ARROW WAS BELIEVED TO BE TIPPED WITH DIAMONDS, GIVING HIM UNPARALLELED MAGICAL POWER.

DIAMOND

Meaning: INVINCIBILITY AND PERMANENCE.

Protective Power: VICTORY OVER ENEMIES.

Birthstone: APRIL.

The ancients believed that diamonds were either the tears of the gods or splinters from falling stars. The Greeks named the diamond *adamas,* meaning "unconquerable." For all their technological achievements (like aqueducts, highways, and concrete buildings), the ancient Romans weren't able to figure out how to cut a diamond. And for them, that was part of its charm.

The Romans loved diamonds for their hardness, not for their sparkle. It was believed that the stone would protect the wearer from mishap and that its protective power would diminish if the stone was altered from its natural state. Roman warriors carried the stone into battle as a talisman to increase their strength. Poor people who couldn't afford to purchase a stone outright could rent them for this purpose.

During the Middle Ages, the diamond came to represent more than just protection. It now stood for constancy in love. The eleventh-century French theologian Marbodeus Gallus wrote that the stone had the power to recall brides to their husbands, while the sixteenth-century physician and gemologist Franciscus Rueus believed the diamond to be the gemstone of reconciliation (especially between husband and wife). This is one power that seems to have extended all the way into the twenty-first century: Many of today's diamond recipients report magically feeling more positive toward their partners.

EIGHTEENTH CENTURY.

NINETEENTH CENTURY.

Despite its growing use in betrothal rings, the diamond didn't become a must-have gem until the eighteenth century. (The seventeenth-century jewelry aficionados were too obsessed with pearls.) Improvements in lighting meant that for the first time, grand events could take place at night. Suddenly no one cared about the stone's hardness; the diamond could pick up the sparkle of a grandly lit ballroom like nothing else. (Adios, pearls!) Looking to capitalize on that twinkle, cutters began to experiment with additional faceting, and the elite responded by wearing diamonds from their hair (tiaras!) to their toes (diamond shoe buckles!).

In the (mostly) pre-credit world of the eighteenth century, jewelry (preferably diamonds!) conveyed social standing, family status, and bank balance. It was like a flash of an Amex black card, but a lot more fun and with a lot more sparkle.

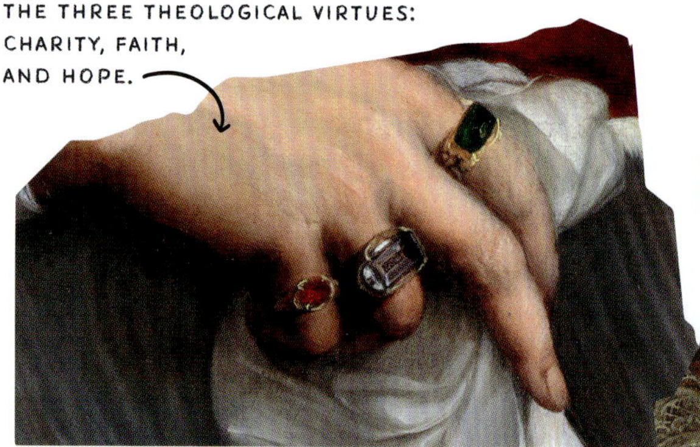

POPE JULIUS II (1443–1513). THE COLORS OF THE RINGS (RED, WHITE, AND GREEN) ARE THOSE OF THE THREE THEOLOGICAL VIRTUES: CHARITY, FAITH, AND HOPE.

MARIA THERESA OF AUSTRIA (1717–1780) (MOTHER OF MARIE ANTOINETTE).

A CROWN OVER A HEART MEANS "LET LOVE RULE."

The Evil Eye shall have no power to harm
Him that shall wear the diamond as a charm.
No monarch shall attempt to thwart his will
And e'en the gods his wishes shall fulfill.

—ORPHIC POEM

IN ANCIENT INDIA, ONLY KINGS WERE PERMITTED TO WEAR DIAMONDS. WOMEN WEREN'T ALLOWED TO WEAR THEM AT ALL—ALLEGEDLY, IT WOULD MAKE THEM UNHAPPY. LOUIS IX OF FRANCE (1214–1270) LIKED THIS IDEA AND PASSED A SIMILAR EDICT RESTRICTING DIAMONDS TO THE KING AND FORBIDDING WOMEN TO WEAR THEM.

A GIRL'S
BEST FRIEND.

D O G

Meaning: DEVOTION, LOYALTY, AND FAITHFULNESS.

Protective Power: A PROTECTOR AND CONSTANT COMPANION WHO WILL PROVIDE HEALING BY LICKING YOUR WOUNDS.

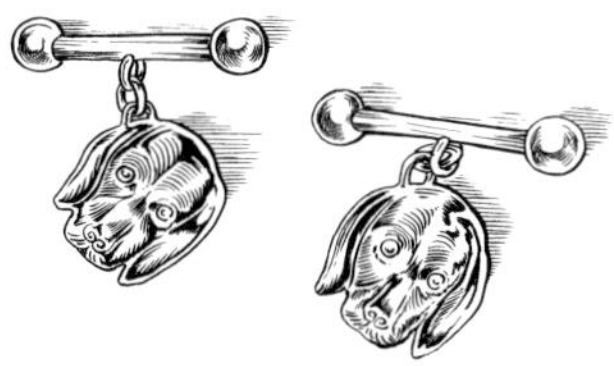

When Versailles was the center of all that was chic and fashionable, lapdogs were the trope of decadent life. Some toy poodles were trained to walk behind their fashionable mistresses, carrying their dress trains in their mouths. A whole chicken intended for her dogs was delivered daily to the bedside of Marie Antoinette. Madame de Maintenon dined with her tiny lapdog Raton, who would share her glass of water. These pampered lapdogs were known as "comforters" and have provided moral support to royal children since the Renaissance. Since high infant mortality rates often meant few siblings, and most royal children were raised in relative isolation due to threat of disease, animals were often a royal child's sole companions.

As these children grew to become the monarchs of Europe, they were utterly devoted pet owners. Queen Victoria commissioned portraits of each of her eighty-eight dogs. Her favorites hung in the royal residence; the rest decorated the walls

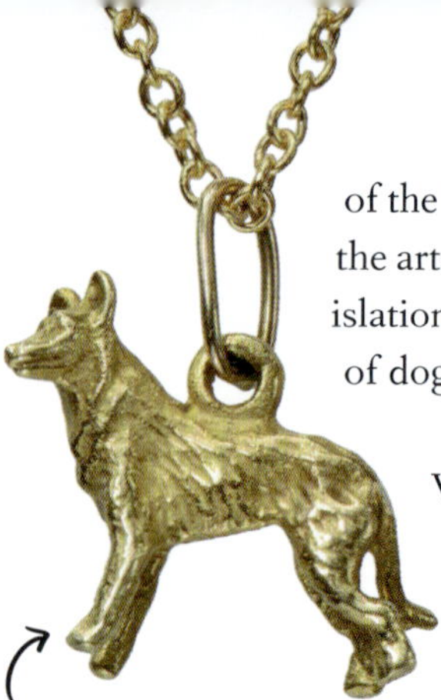

CIRCA 1960. COURTESY OF ERIE BASIN.

of the kennel. The queen's passion for her animals wasn't confined to the arts. She personally ensured the passage of animal protective legislation, and the example set by her ardor created an enduring nation of dog lovers.

Dog-themed jewelry was an equal opportunity affair: Women and men adorned themselves with likenesses of their favorite breeds through brooches, cuff links, and tie pins. A beloved canine companion could be commemorated by jewels encasing one's hair. In 1863, the Prince of Wales commissioned a crystal (a reversed crystal intaglio) of the queen's much-loved collie Gypsey, who had recently died.

BABY PRINCESS ALICE (1843–1878) WATCHED OVER BY DANDIE. THE PAINTING WAS A SURPRISE GIFT FROM PRINCE ALBERT TO QUEEN VICTORIA.

ROMAN BRONZE DOG BROOCH.

BOY WITH BLACK SPANIEL, CIRCA 1767.

A MINIATURE PORTRAIT PAINTED BY THE NINETEENTH-CENTURY BOSTON ARTIST CLARISSA PETER RUSSELLS.

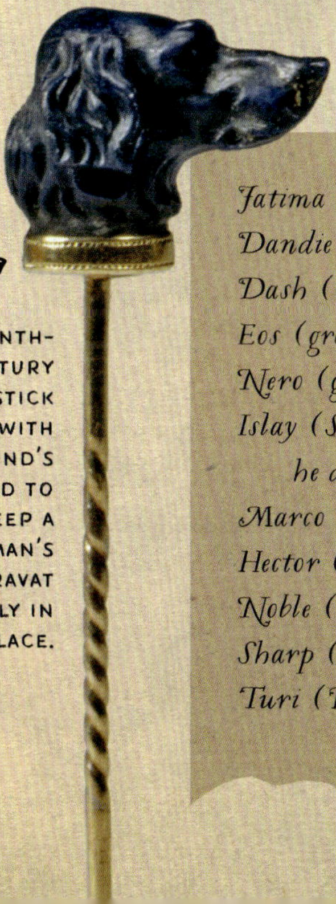

NINETEENTH-CENTURY STICK PIN WITH HOUND'S HEAD TO KEEP A GENTLEMAN'S CRAVAT FIRMLY IN PLACE.

QUEEN VICTORIA'S DOGS:

Fatima (pug)
Dandie (Skye terrier)
Dash (Cavalier King Charles spaniel)
Eos (greyhound brought by Prince Albert from Germany)
Nero (greyhound)
Islay (Skye terrier—Victoria owned Islay for five years and he died after losing a fight with a cat)
Marco (small spitz, the first of her many Pomeranians)
Hector (deerhound)
Noble (the queen's favorite collie)
Sharp (collie)
Turi (Pomeranian, who lay on her deathbed at her request)

A WHITE DOVE
IS AN ANGEL,
READY TO TAKE A
SOUL TO HEAVEN.
NINETEENTH
CENTURY.

D O V E

Meaning: PEACE, HOPE, AND LOVE.

Protective Power: HEALING QUARRELS AND UNITING FRIENDS.

In ancient Mesopotamia, doves were the symbols of Inanna-Ishtar, goddess of love, sexuality, and war. The bird was subsequently associated with her Greek and Roman equivalents (Aphrodite and Venus), until it was appropriated as a symbol of peace and love by Judaism, Islam, and Christianity.

The dove had a big design moment in 1737, when a Roman mosaic depicting the birds drinking water was uncovered at Hadrian's Villa. The subject and the mosaic technique inspired artists and designers all over Europe. The dove proved a particularly popular subject for micromosaics, a type of mosaic technique that uses tiny glass pieces, or tesserae, to create a design. Micromosaics set in rings, pendants, and brooches were a favorite souvenir of British tourists on their Grand Tour through Italy. The antique jewelry collector Alessandro Michele, who was creative director at Gucci for many years before moving to Valentino, used antique micromosaics in his contemporary fine jewelry collection for Gucci. (It was Alessandro who introduced the pop icon Harry Styles to micromosaics.)

In the sentimental Victorian age, doves were a favorite motif for pendants and brooches. A dove holding an olive branch symbolized hope, friendship, and peace. When it held a heart in its beak, it symbolized love.

THE FRENCH "SAINT ESPRIT," OR HOLY SPIRIT DOVE, DESCENDING FROM HEAVEN TO EARTH WITH WINGS SPREAD. IT IS A SYMBOL OF FAITH AND BRINGS LUCK TO THE WEARER. CIRCA 1820. COURTESY OF INEZ STODEL.

BELIEVED TO MATE FOR LIFE, DOVES SYMBOLIZED MARITAL LOVE. NINETEENTH CENTURY.

ANCIENT GREEK DOVE EARRING.

MICROMOSAIC PENDANT MADE OF TINY PIECES OF INLAID GLASS, CIRCA 1860. COURTESY OF ERIE BASIN.

FOUR-YEAR-OLD PRINCESS MAUD (1869–1938) (GRANDDAUGHTER OF QUEEN VICTORIA) WEARING A TINY DOVE NECKLACE.

ANCIENT GOLD PIN TOPPED WITH A DOVE USED TO HOLD A WOMAN'S HAIR IN PLACE OR TO SECURE HER DRESS AT THE SHOULDERS.

The French "Saint Esprit" or Holy Spirit dove is depicted descending from heaven to earth with wings spread. This is a symbol of faith and was meant to bring luck to the wearer.

PAIR OF STOVE DOVES, 350–300 B.C.

ZEUS IN THE FORM OF AN EAGLE, CARRYING THE TROJAN PRINCE GANYMEDE TO MOUNT OLYMPUS TO BE A CUP-BEARER FOR THE GODS.

EAGLE

Meaning: POWER, STRENGTH, AND ROYALTY.

Protective Power: SACRED MESSENGERS OF THE CREATOR, GUARDIAN SPIRITS, AND GUIDING FORCES.

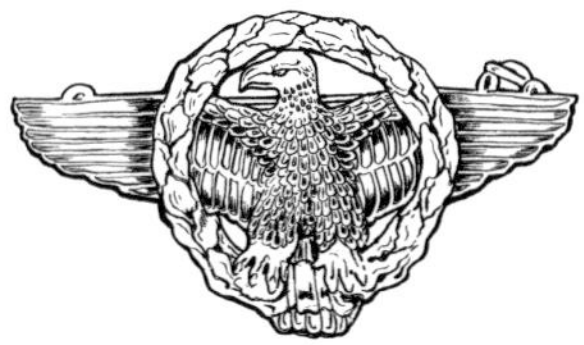

The eagle was the symbol of Zeus, and still represents power and majesty. Its massive wingspan commands attention. The Roman Empire, masters of branding, adopted the eagle as the world's first logo, a symbol of their military might. An image of the eagle appeared above the letters SPQR: Senatus Populusque Romanus (the senate and people of Rome). One was carried by the *aquilifer* (eagle-bearer) and was considered the most important possession of the legion; its loss was a disgrace.

In the chivalric medieval period, the eagle became a recognizable symbol of power and pedigree. The first Holy Roman emperor, Charlemagne, incorporated the eagle into his coat of arms in 800.

The eagle was the personal symbol for Roman-obsessed Napoleon. And the United States took the eagle as its national symbol in 1782. It wasn't a generic eagle—this was the North American bald eagle. The bird was sacred in some Native American cultures, such as the Lakota (who give an eagle feather as a symbol of honor) and the Choctaw (who consider the eagle to be a symbol of peace).

EIGHTEENTH-CENTURY DESIGN DEPICTING AN EAGLE ATOP A ROMAN STANDARD.

After her wedding ceremony in 1840, Queen Victoria presented each of her twelve train-bearers (the aristocratic women who held the train of her dress) a brooch designed by her new husband, Prince Albert. The gold brooches are slightly different from one another but each features an eagle, the symbol of the House of Coburg, set with a turquoise body and outstretched wings, a diamond beak, and round ruby eyes, with pearls grasped tightly in its talons. Each gem was selected for its symbolism: turquoise blue to evoke the color of forget-me-nots, rubies as symbols of passion, diamonds representing eternity, and pearls for true love. The gift was a break from the tradition of gifting a dove of Venus to the wedding party; the Coburg Eagle was chosen to honor the bridegroom's family.

THIRD CENTURY.

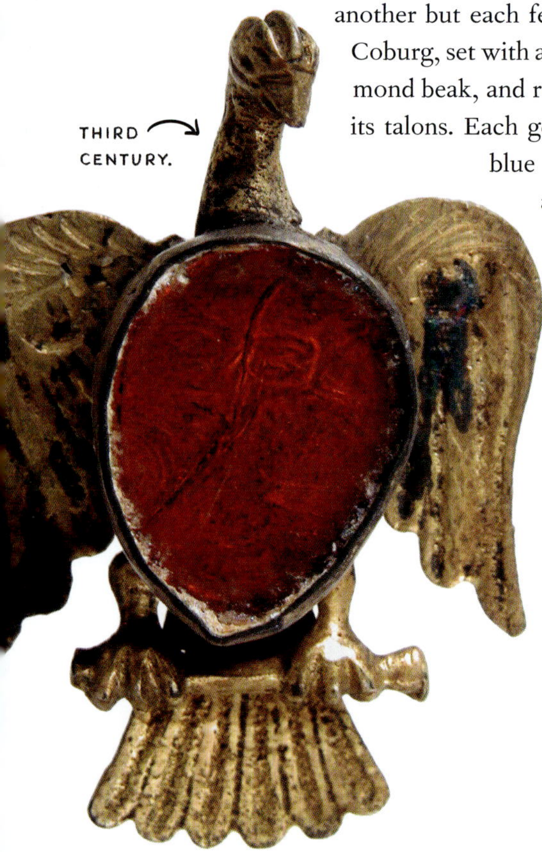

THIS EAGLE IS ONE OF THE TWELVE THAT WERE GIVEN TO QUEEN VICTORIA'S BRIDESMAIDS. IT'S AN EXAMPLE OF THE COUPLE'S LOVE OF JEWELRY AND SENTIMENTALITY.

IN ANCIENT EGYPT, THE EAGLE REPRESENTED STRENGTH AND DIVINITY. NINETEENTH CENTURY.

Eagle jewelry can be traced to the Neanderthals, who used eagle talons to create pendants.

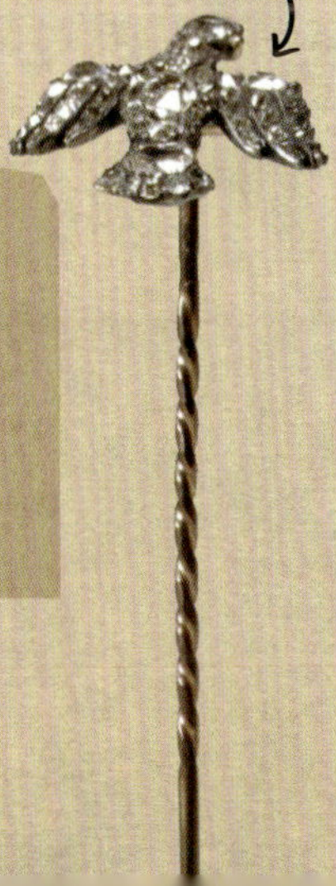

NINETEENTH-CENTURY STICK PIN.

THIS ELEPHANT BELONGED TO THE SEVENTEENTH-CENTURY MUGHAL EMPEROR JAHANGIR (1569–1627), AND WAS NAMED ALAM GUMAN, WHICH TRANSLATES TO "THE ARROGANT ONE OF THE EARTH."

ELEPHANT

Meaning: ROYALTY; BRINGER OF RAIN, GOOD FORTUNE, AND FERTILITY.

Protective Power: WARDS OFF NEGATIVE ENERGY.

Elephants are revered in India as sacred symbols of strength, wisdom, and peace. In Hindu mythology, the earth is supported by four elephants standing on the back of a turtle. And Ganesha, the elephant-headed god, is the remover of all obstacles, the patron of wisdom and new beginnings. In Buddhism, the white elephant is a sacred symbol of purity and compassion, as Buddha's mother dreamt of a white elephant just before his birth. For ancient Romans, this large mammal symbolized strength and prowess in war after Hannibal, the Carthaginian general, led his army, including war elephants, across the Alps into Italy. (The elephants were used as psychological weapons to instill fear into the Roman troops.)

In Victorian jewelry, elephants with their trunks raised symbolized good luck and prosperity. Miniature glass elephants, just the right size to be tucked into a pocket, were marketed with the tagline "The Lucky Elephant that brings luck."

In the fifteenth century, Christian V of Denmark created the Order of the Elephant, equivalent to knighthood and the highest-ranking honor in the nation. Upon induction into the order, one is given a white enamel elephant pendant to wear. The Danish royal family has been relatively stingy in awarding the Order of the Elephant, although they do love to give it to each other (and other royal friends). In fact, members of the Danish royal family are born Knights of the Order and receive their insignia on significant occasions. When King Frederik X and Queen Mary ascended the throne in January 2024, they both wore their Order of the Elephant collar and badge.

Luckily for the rest of us, the Danish royal family doesn't have a monopoly on the elephant's image or the good luck it will bring.

THE ELEPHANT AND CAMELLIA BLOSSOMS SYMBOLIZE THE TEACHING OF WISDOM. COURTESY OF CECE JEWELLERY.

THIS PENDANT BELONGED TO THE FRENCH KING LOUIS XVIII (1755–1824).

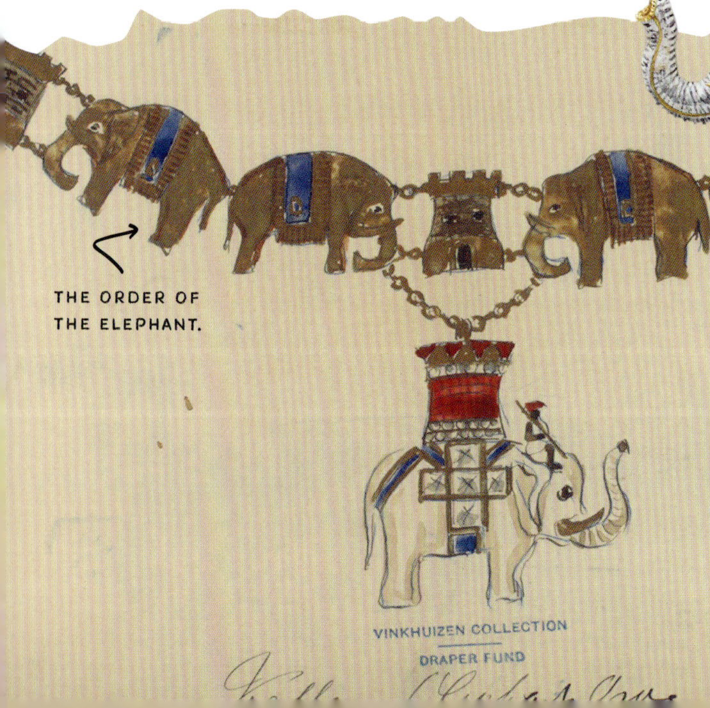

THE ORDER OF THE ELEPHANT.

CARTIER HAPPY ELEPHANT LUCKY CHARM, 1975. COURTESY OF INEZ STODEL.

In Feng Shui, elephants are revered, as they help accumulate good chi, promote blessings, and protect from harmful energy.

SWEDISH ASTRONOMER TYCHO BRAHE WEARING THE ORDER OF THE ELEPHANT, 1596.

CARTIER ELEPHANT BRACELET. COURTESY OF INEZ STODEL.

DANCING ELEPHANT EARRINGS, CIRCA NINETEENTH CENTURY.

MAHARAJA SHER SINGH (1807–1843). ANCIENT INDIAN PHILOSOPHERS SAID THAT OFFERING AN EMERALD TO A GOD WOULD GRANT ONE THE KNOWLEDGE OF THE SOUL AND ETERNAL LIFE.

EMERALD

Meaning: HOPE AND PROSPERITY.

Protective Power: PROVIDES PROTECTION FOR TRAVELERS ON JOURNEYS.

Birthstone: MAY.

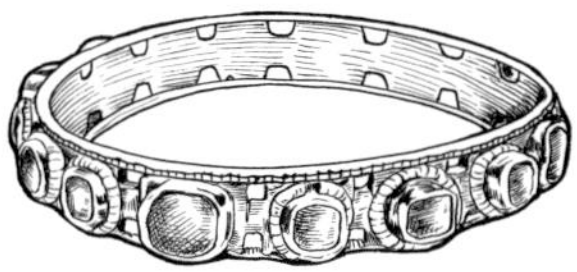

Emeralds are known as the unownable stones. While they might lend themselves to the wearer, history shows that eventually they will be lost, cracked, stolen, or taken in some other way. According to legend, the first emerald in the universe was the chief stone in Satan's crown, and even he couldn't hold on to it. When he was cast out of heaven and into hell, the stone slipped out of his circlet and tumbled to earth.

Alexander the Great, who managed to conquer the entire known world, also couldn't maintain a hold on his emerald. He wore a large emerald in his belt (presumably obtained during his invasion of India), and while he was bathing in the Euphrates River, a snake leapt out of the water and bit it right off. Alexander died soon after.

In the sixteenth century, the Spanish conquistador Hernán Cortés was ruthless in his pursuit of wealth (and his destruction of the indigenous peoples of the Americas). After one expedition, he brought back to Spain five great emeralds, which had been carved by the Aztecs into various shapes including fish and flowers, likely looted from the treasures of Montezuma. Cortés was so captivated by their brilliance that he refused to sell them, for any price. Instead, he gave them to his wife, which offended Queen Isabella, who desired them for herself.

There was good reason for all this fuss over the South American emeralds: No prior source (most in circulation originated from Egypt) could compete with Colombian emeralds for size, color, or clarity. Due in part to his refusal to part with the stones, Cortés fell out of favor with the Spanish court. Cortés went on to be shipwrecked in 1541; he survived, but the emeralds were lost at sea.

The moral of the emerald story is that when loved and cherished, an emerald is said to bring luck; when neglected or lost, it can take alarming revenge.

"CROWN OF THE ANDES" WITH FOUR HUNDRED UNTREATED COLONIAL EMERALDS. THIS CROWN WAS MADE IN THE SIXTEENTH CENTURY BY SPANIARDS TO ADORN A STATUE OF THE VIRGIN MARY.

IN ANCIENT LORE, EMERALDS WERE THOUGHT TO GRANT SAFE TRAVEL.

ROMAN NECKLACE WITH EMERALD BEADS.

EMERALDS WITH A VIBRANT GRASS-GREEN COLOR ARE DUBBED MUZO GREEN (EVEN IF THEY WERE NOT MINED IN MUZO, COLOMBIA, THE EMERALD CAPITAL OF THE WORLD).

ANCIENT EGYPTIANS REVERED THE EMERALD FOR ITS GREEN COLOR. GREEN, THE COLOR OF THE PAPYRUS PLANT, SYMBOLIZED LIFE. MUMMIES WERE GIVEN PAPYRUS-SHAPED SCEPTERS STUDDED WITH EMERALDS.

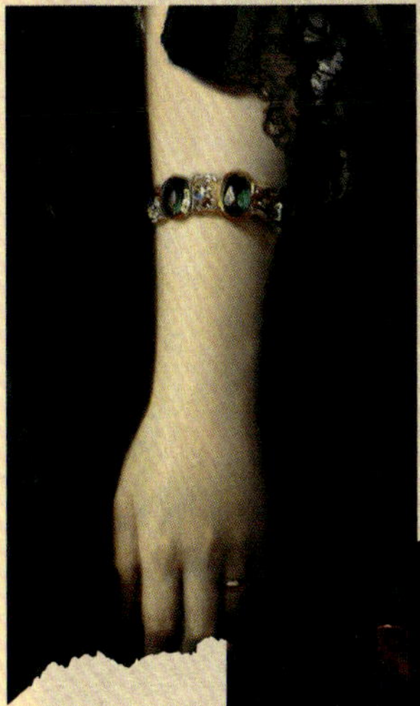

EMERALD RING WORN BY NAPOLEON BONAPARTE'S YOUNGER BROTHER, CIRCA 1800.

AN EMERALD HAS THE POWER TO FORESHADOW THINGS TO COME.

Dreaming of an emerald means the renewal of a friendship and a bright future.

ANCIENT EGYPTIAN EYE AMULET.
THE EYE REPRESENTS THE LEFT EYE
OF THE GOD HORUS, WHICH HAD BEEN
LOST IN BATTLE AND WAS MAGICALLY
RESTORED BY THE FALCON GOD HATHOR.

E Y E

Meaning: THE AMULETIC EYE WATCHES WHERE THE HUMAN EYE CANNOT.

Protective Power: PREVENTS THE CURSE OF AN ENVIOUS, MALEVOLENT GLARE.

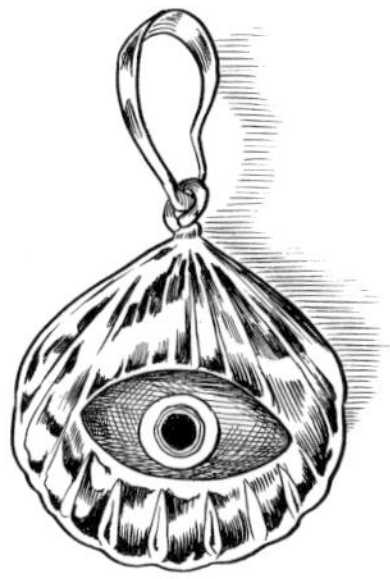

Many of the unexplainable mishaps in the ancient world were attributed to a malignant force called the evil eye. Its power was summoned by a malevolent glare—usually when the recipient was oblivious to it. Historians think the concept dates back five thousand years. The evil eye was the harbinger of ill health and poor fortune. It's hard to overstate how worrisome it was for our ancestors. During the Black Death in the fourteenth century, disease was supposedly transmitted by a look from a sick person. Amulets offered the only known protection.

LATE NINETEENTH CENTURY.

SURREALIST ITALIAN EYE STICK PIN. COURTESY OF BELL AND BIRD.

The most powerful talisman against the evil eye was thought to be another eye. Arab culture employs a blue glass eye-like charm known as a *nazar*, or "sight" in Arabic, to ward off wickedness; the logic is literally "an eye for an eye." The *nazar* acts as a magical boomerang, sending maliciousness right back to the evil deliverer. Nearly every ancient culture around the world had some version of this. Glass beads were introduced in the Mediterranean in about 1500 B.C., and evil-eye beads were manufactured almost as soon as glass technology made it possible.

Perhaps some of the credit for the modern obsession with the evil eye should be given to the Greek jewelry designer Ileana Makri. Her 1999 jewelry collection included sapphire and diamond evil eye charms; when the hip New York City department store Barneys picked up her line, the symbol was introduced to a new audience. Many other modern jewelers have been similarly inspired to create their own version of this ancient, protective talisman.

CIRCA 1950S. COURTESY OF ERIE BASIN.

INDIAN GOLD BANGLE WITH A GLASS EVIL EYE CHARM, NINETEENTH CENTURY.

ILEANA MAKRI PAVÉ-SET RING.

TURKISH AMULET WITH THE ARABIC MOTTO; 'MA SHA' ALLAH' (AS GOD WILLS). CIRCA TWENTIETH CENTURY.

> *"There is nothing more dreaded by the people, nor considered more deadly in its effects, than the Evil Eye."*
>
> —LADY JANE FRANCESCA WILDE (OSCAR'S MOTHER), *ANCIENT LEGENDS, MYSTIC CHARMS AND SUPERSTITIONS OF IRELAND* (1887)

ANCIENT EGYPTIAN STRING OF EYE BEADS.

VICTORIAN GARNETS WERE OFTEN CALLED BOHEMIAN GARNETS, NAMED AFTER THE AREA MOST OF THEM WERE MINED. (NOW MODERN-DAY CZECH REPUBLIC).

GARNET

Meaning: A STONE OF GOOD MAGIC; BRINGS PROTECTION AND FRIENDSHIP.

Protective Power: PLACED UNDER A PILLOW, A GARNET CAN WARD OFF DEMONS AND NIGHTMARES.

Birthstone: JANUARY.

According to Indian mythology, all gems were formed when the gods dismembered the demon Vala. The garnet came from his toenail. When medieval Europeans saw the garnet, they got less of a toenail vibe and more of a seed one. The name *garnet* comes from medieval Latin for *granatus*, meaning "seed or pomegranate."

Garnet was known as the passion stone for its ability to inflame sexual energy. However, beware that staring too long at a garnet may cause anger or unhealthy passions to arise. Avoiding that libidinous tightrope, a garnet gifted in platonic friendship ensures loyalty and faithfulness. The stone's pomegranate resemblance links it to the myth of Demeter and Persephone: Mother and daughter separated when Hades took Demeter to be his bride in the underworld. The pair were reunited after Demeter ate pomegranate seeds.

In the ancient world, wearing a garnet around one's neck was thought to chase any blue feelings away. The belief in the power of garnets to illuminate had cross-cultural appeal. In Scandinavia, garnets were buried with the dead to light them on their path to the next world. In Talmudic legend, Noah illuminated the ark with a giant garnet. According to the Qu'ran, the light of the garnet illuminates the fourth heaven. Some claimed that the stone couldn't be hidden under clothing because its light would shine through. A quick experiment will prove that wrong, but the jury is still out on whether it will ward off nightmares, as medieval travelers believed.

SEVENTH-CENTURY RING.

ANCIENT GREEK. WEARING GARNETS AROUND THE NECK WAS THOUGHT TO KEEP DEPRESSION AWAY.

PORTRAIT OF KATARZYNA JAHN, THE ARTIST'S SISTER, IN 1849.

Stolen garnets bring bad luck to the thief until the jewels are returned.

According to ancient lore, Capricorns should wear no other gems than garnets, and in doing so will ensure faithfulness in love and true friendship from all others.

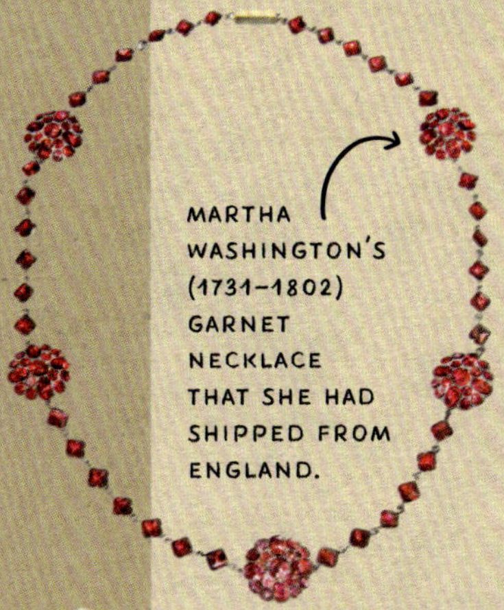

MARTHA WASHINGTON'S (1731–1802) GARNET NECKLACE THAT SHE HAD SHIPPED FROM ENGLAND.

ANCIENT GREEKS LOVED A MATCHING SET. GARNET EARRINGS AND NECKLACE EACH SET WITH A LARGE GARNET CABOCHON, FIRST CENTURY B.C.

THE BRITISH COLONIST MARY ELIZABETH BELLINGER ELLIOTT (1751–1774) WEARING GARNETS IN HER 1766 WEDDING PORTRAIT.

ALUMINIUM HAMSA AMULET, TWENTIETH CENTURY.

HAND (SINGLE)

Meaning: PROTECTIVE AND GOOD FORTUNE.

Protective Power: PROTECTS AGAINST ILL WILL AND THE EVIL EYE.

Represented in some of the earliest cave drawings, the human hand is one of our most ancient symbols of human consciousness. In many spiritual and healing traditions, it is considered a conduit of power. The laying-on of hands is a means of blessing and healing. Hands have been used as amulets for thousands of years. In life, an ancient Egyptian might have only worn one or two amulets, but in death, mummies were festooned in protective charms to ensure all parts of the body were resurrected in the afterlife. The hand was right at the top of that list.

HAMSA HAND

An open hand figures in both Jewish and Islamic cultures. This symmetrical hand, with a thumb on either side, is known as the hamsa hand, derived from the Hebrew word for "five," *hamesh*.

INDIAN HAMSA, LATE EIGHTEENTH CENTURY.

MANO FIGA

A clenched hand, with a thumb poking out between the first and second fingers, is a *mano fisco*, a powerful talisman against the evil eye (see Eye, page 111). In Etruria, ancient Italy, the sign was an obscene gesture. *Figa*, or *fig*, was a slang term for female genitalia, and the hand sign was a reference to heterosexual sex. The obscenity was intended to distract and divert the evil eye. Roman soldiers often carried the protective symbol along with a phallic amulet—to cover all their bases.

FIGA HAND CHARM, CIRCA 1980. COURTESY OF ERIE BASIN.

MANO CORNUTO

A mano cornuto is a hand making the "sign of the horns." Some historians theorized that the sign is a reference to the neopagan worship of a fertility goddess, whose husband was the Horned God. Others think that the sacredness of the head of a horned animal (likely a bull) derives from its resemblance to the female genitals. Even its use at heavy metal concerts can be traced back to the Mediterranean, where it was used to ward off the evil eye. According to rock lore, Ronnie James Dio of Black Sabbath is credited with popularizing the sign today. He said he learned it from his Italian grandmother.

MANO CORNUTO IN TURQUOISE, EARLY-NINETEENTH CENTURY. COURTESY OF INEZ STODEL.

SILVER NECKLACE WITH THE "HAND OF FATIMAH." NEARLY IDENTICAL TO THE HAMSA HAND, THIS VERSION IS USED IN ISLAMIC CONTEXT. FATIMAH WAS THE DAUGHTER OF MUHAMMAD, FOUNDER OF ISLAM.

A CHAIN OF AMULETIC SYMBOLS INCLUDING A HAMSA HAND.

SEVENTEENTH-CENTURY GLASS SPANISH PENDANT CARVED FROM ROCK CRYSTAL.

CIRCA 1332–1322 B.C.

The word "manifestation" is derived from the Latin word for hand, manus.

MARIA ANNA OF SPAIN (1606–1646), HOLY ROMAN EMPRESS, PROTECTED BY A CORAL HAND AT FIVE MONTHS OLD.

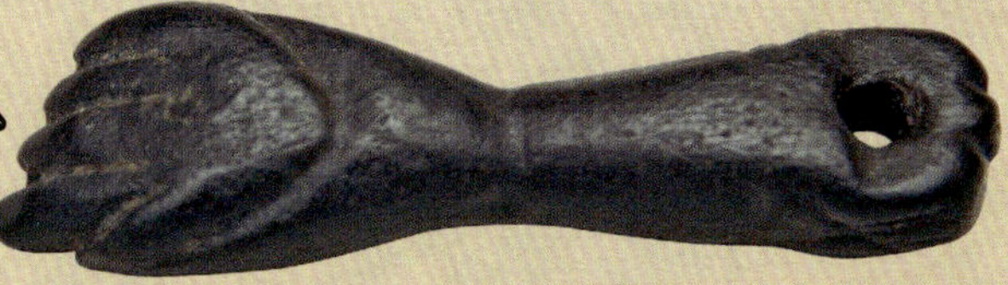

THIS PROTECTIVE AMULET WAS PINNED ON A SMALL BOY WHO WAS LEFT AT THE FOUNDLING HOSPITAL IN LONDON IN 1756.

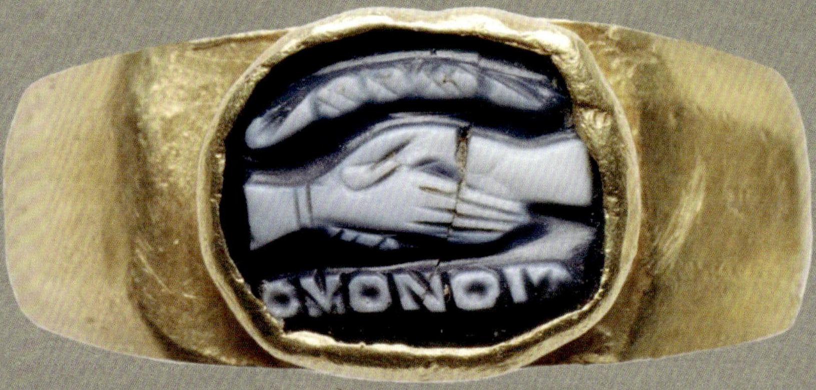

THE PAIRED HANDS ARE FRAMED BY A GARLAND OF FLOWERS ABOVE AND THE GREEK WORD *OMONOIA* ("HARMONY") BELOW, THIRD CENTURY A.D.

HANDS (PAIR)

Meaning: LOYALTY, ROMANCE, FAITH, AND FIDELITY.

Protective Power: FAITHFULLY BINDS A COUPLE TOGETHER.

In ancient Rome, handshakes were not everyday greetings. They were a ritualistic gesture: to seal a deal or pledge an oath or bind a marriage. It was also customary to exchange rings to commemorate an agreement. A *fede* ring with a pair of hands clasped together alluded to the agreement between a betrothed couple. The motif of conjoined hands continued through the Middle Ages and into the Renaissance, when a new type of *fede* ring was developed: the gimmel ring. The name comes from the Latin for "twin" because the ring comes apart in two halves. During the engagement, it was common for the hoops to be separated, each person wearing a half. On the wedding day, the halves were reunited for the bride to wear as a wedding band. To this day, the term *fede* is still synonymous with wedding rings in Italy.

The two-hand concept resonated with eighteenth-century British couples so much that jewelers adapted the style to feature the fashionable lace cuffs of the era. In a very meta move, some hands even wore their own rings. These rings didn't come apart but swiveled open to reveal one or two hearts hidden behind the hands.

When it comes to hands and heart, the Irish Claddagh ring, with its romantic creation story, tops the list. In the seventeenth century, shortly before he was due to be married, an Irish fisherman named Richard Joyce was en route to the West Indies when he was captured by Algerian pirates and sold into slavery. He was purchased by a goldsmith, who taught him the craft. Thinking of his love at home, Richard created the first Claddagh ring. In 1689, after an agreement with King William III to release all his subjects held in slavery, Richard Joyce returned home to Galway. His sweetheart had waited, and the two were married with the Claddagh serving as their wedding band.

EARLY-SEVENTEENTH-CENTURY ENGLISH *FEDE* RING INSCRIBED WITH "THINKE OF ME."

IN CLADDAGH RINGS, A HEART MEANS LOVE, A CROWN MEANS LOYALTY, AND TWO CLASPED HANDS REPRESENT FRIENDSHIP.

MOURNING RING, CIRCA LATE NINETEENTH CENTURY.

Handfasting, where the hands of the couple are tied together with a cord or ribbon, was a British betrothal ritual that was practiced in England until the eighteenth century and continued in Scotland until the twentieth.

The right hand was considered sacred to the goddess of fidelity, Fides.

BRACELET HANDS, 1854.

SIBYLLE OF CLEVES, SIXTEENTH-CENTURY NOBLEWOMAN AND OLDER SISTER OF ANNE OF CLEVES (HENRY VIII'S FOURTH WIFE).

HEART

Meaning: LOVE AND AFFECTION.

Protective Powers: GUARDS AGAINST NEGATIVITY.

The first double-clefted hearts were little more than decorative doodles—likely cribbed from nature—on the edges of medieval manuscripts. Medieval Europe, with a mostly illiterate population, was all about symbols. During the thirteenth and fourteenth centuries, this random shape began to signify love—and has been a symbol of love ever since.

In part to escape the drudgery of daily existence (know the feeling?), medieval folks created a rich fantasy life centered around love. This was the era that birthed the story of King Arthur and the Knights of the Round Table. True love was chivalric. The greatest knight wasn't just a warrior; he was kind, courteous, and devoted to his lady.

In sixteenth-century Scotland, a silver open heart-shaped brooch was a common betrothal gift. After the couple married and had a child, the brooch would be pinned to the baby's clothes to ward off witches or even worse, some evil fairies who might steal the baby and switch it out (this was known as a changeling. Yikes!).

By the eighteenth century, the heart had become an established symbol for all kinds of love. And in the nineteenth century, jewelry-loving Queen Victoria kept the heart trend front and center. She loved jewelry with some sentimentality, and the heart fit that bill perfectly. She wore hearts both during the happy periods of her life and in mourning.

A HEART WITH A CROWN REPRESENTS LOYALTY.

WHEN A HEART'S TAIL CURVES TO THE RIGHT, IT'S KNOWN AS A "WITCH'S HEART" AND MEANS "BEWITCHED BY LOVE."

FIFTEENTH-CENTURY UNICORN HEART RING.

ANNA MARIA LERGETPORER BY BARBARA KRAFFT (WHO BECAME FAMOUS FOR PAINTING MOZART), 1811.

Ancient Egyptians believed the heart, not the brain, was the center of the mind, intellect, emotions, and memory.

IT IS A SWEDISH TRADITION TO GIVE AN INFANT GIRL A HEART PENDANT AS A CHRISTENING GIFT.

THE ACTOR JOHN DREW, JR. (1853–1927) (GREAT-GREAT-UNCLE TO DREW BARRYMORE), WEARING A HORSESHOE TIE PIN.

HORSESHOE

Meaning: Good luck, protection, and strength.

Protective Powers: Wards off evil spirits and negative energy. The power to overcome obstacles.

At a time when the Roman Empire spanned three continents, first-century Romans began worshipping Epona as a protector of horses and the patroness of the Roman cavalry. She was the only Celtic deity ever venerated in Rome. For the Celts, she was the goddess of fertility as well as a protector of horses. In addition to the goddess, the Romans adopted the Celtic practice of protecting hooves with nailed-on shoes.

It wasn't until the tenth century that the horseshoe was tied to luck. According to legend, an English blacksmith named Dunstan was crafting horseshoes when the devil entered the forge, demanding his horse be reshod. Dunstan caused the devil great pain by either nailing iron shoes on him or by twisting his nose with hot tongs (the method of torture changes depending on the source of the story). But Dunstan's triumph over the devil forever imbued the horseshoe with a supernatural positive vibe.

CIRCA 1900. COURTESY OF ERIE BASIN.

In the nineteenth century, the horseshoe became more than a lucky charm: It evolved into a symbol of passion for equestrian sports, particularly horse racing. In Britain, the legacy of horse racing dates to Roman conquest. The fashion for racing spread to France after Napoleon III was exiled to London in the 1830s and caught the horse racing bug. He encouraged the French adoption of the sport, and in 1857, the first Paris Grand Prix was run at Longchamp in the Bois de Boulogne.

Horseshoe jewelry became a fashionable nod to equestrian sports, as well as a popular token for both platonic relationships and romantic ones. It conveyed affection and a wish for good fortune.

HORSEHOOF LOCKET. COURTESY OF BELL AND BIRD.

LADY ALEXANDRINA, NINETEENTH-CENTURY IRISH ARISTOCRAT.

HORSESHOE DIAMOND BRACELET. COURTESY OF BELL AND BIRD.

Part of the luck of the horseshoe is its seven nails. Humans have considered the number seven to be lucky for thousands of years.

EMPRESS EUGÉNIE.

RUBY HORSESHOE PENDANT. COURTESY OF BELL AND BIRD.

VICTORIAN-ERA BRACELET. COURTESY OF ERIE BASIN.

THERE IS ALSO A MEXICAN FOLK TRADITION OF WEARING DEAD HUMMINGBIRDS. THESE CHARMS (NOW ILLEGAL), KNOWN AS CHUPAROSAS, ARE LOVE TALISMANS.

HUMMINGBIRD

Meaning: JOY, ENERGY, AND RESILIENCE.

Protective Power: POWER OF LOVE TO REVERSE TIME AND CHANGE THE COURSE OF FATE.

Hummingbirds exist only in the Americas. When Spanish explorers saw the birds for the first time, they were so amazed by their iridescent plumage they dubbed them *joyas voladoras*, or "flying jewels."

The hummingbird is a central character in many Native American mythological tribal stories as a symbol of courage and resilience. In Mayan culture, it was revered as a magical being, the hummingbird being the sun in disguise. In Hopi and Zuni legends, the hummingbirds intervened with the gods on behalf of humans to summon the rainy season. Pueblo Indians have hummingbird dances and use the birds' feathers to bring rain. The Inca believed the hummingbird was a messenger from heaven. The Aztec believed the bird's iridescent feathers were created from the sun's rays. The hummingbird was thought to be symbolic of the warrior god Huitzilopochtli; warriors who died in battle were supposedly reincarnated as hummingbird messengers between the living and the dead.

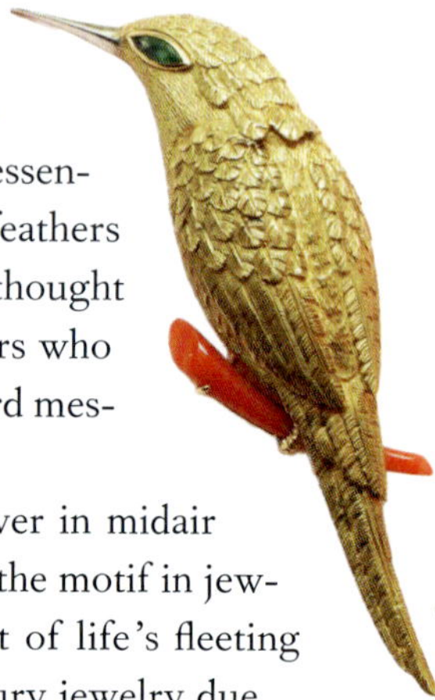

HUMMINGBIRD FROM THE FRENCH JEWELRY HOUSE VAN CLEEF & ARPELS, CIRCA 1950. COURTESY OF INEZ STODEL.

The hummingbird's vibrant colors and ability to hover in midair also captured the imagination of the Victorians, who used the motif in jewelry to represent vivacity, playfulness, and the enjoyment of life's fleeting moments. It was the most popular bird in nineteenth-century jewelry due to its colorful iridescent plumage.

Unfortunately, some Victorians took the moniker of "flying jewels" literally, wearing taxidermied hummingbirds as necklaces and earrings. If sporting dead hummingbirds seems a bit too gruesome, know that many other Victorians agreed. Some society women were so appalled by the practice that they were galvanized to start bird protection organizations throughout Europe and the United States. The work of their organizations, forerunners of our Audubon Societies, led to banning the feather trade.

A PLATE FROM "ART FORMS OF NATURE" BY GERMAN BIOLOGIST AND ILLUSTRATOR ERNST HAECKEL, 1904.

THE AZTEC SUN GOD, HUITZILOPOCHTLI, WAS SAID TO BE BORN FROM HUMMINGBIRD FEATHERS THAT FELL FROM THE SKY.

See it darting through the air almost as quick as thought!—now it is within a yard of your face!—in an instant gone!—now it flutters from flower to flower to sip the silver dew—it is now a ruby—now a topaz—now an emerald—now all burnished gold!

—CHARLES WATERTON ON THE HUMMINGBIRD, AFTER TRAVELING THROUGH LATIN AMERICA IN THE EARLY NINETEENTH CENTURY

1950s DIAMOND HUMMINGBIRD WITH RUBY EYES. COURTESY OF ERIE BASIN.

THE TWENTIETH-CENTURY PORTRAIT ARTIST PHILIP DE LÁZLÓ WAS SO ENAMORED OF JADE THAT THAT HE BOUGHT HIS OWN JADE JEWELRY FOR HIS SOCIALITE SUBJECTS TO WEAR.

J A D E

Meaning: THE STONE OF HEAVEN.

Protective Power: CAN ABSORB BAD LUCK.

ALTERNATE MARCH BIRTHSTONE.

According to ancient Chinese legend, jade was believed to be the congealed semen of the Celestial Dragon from its union with Mother Earth. Touching jade would bring one into concert with that mystical dragon. Known as the stone of heaven, jade specimens with the most translucent green color were confiscated by the Chinese royal family, hence the name "imperial jade." Obviously it was thought that jade was a masculine force, given the whole Celestial Dragon thing, so the search for jade was conducted primarily by women, thought to attract the stone with their feminine energy.

In China, jade has been imbued with almost every virtue, from peace and serenity to good luck and wealth. In ancient China, it was *the* gift for nearly every situation. Girl comes of age? Jade phoenix. Newly engaged? How about a jade butterfly for good fortune. Newlyweds? Jade unicorn with rider. Male best friends forever? Jade amulets. The list goes on.

There is no relationship in the gem world that exists quite like the Chinese and jade. But other cultures did believe in its curative power. The ancient Egyptians would tie jade to the arm or leg as a healing stone. The ancient Greeks believed it to be a remedy for stomach ailments. The Mayans considered it a living stone and used it in funeral rituals. Jade amulets were carried as lucky charms in late Victorian England. Archibald Primrose, fifth Earl of Rosebery, and Leopold de Rothschild sparked a jade craze among the horsey set after both gentlemen carried amulets when their Thoroughbreds won the Derby (Lord Rosebery's horse Ladas won the Epsom Derby in 1894, and Rothschild's horse St. Amant won it in 1904).

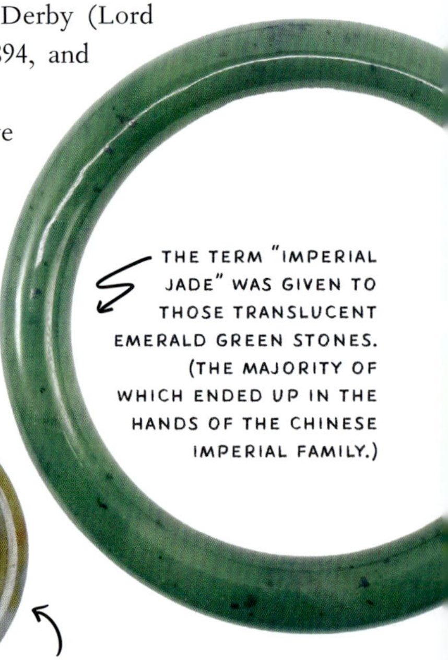

THE TERM "IMPERIAL JADE" WAS GIVEN TO THOSE TRANSLUCENT EMERALD GREEN STONES. (THE MAJORITY OF WHICH ENDED UP IN THE HANDS OF THE CHINESE IMPERIAL FAMILY.)

To this day, many people around the world believe in the power of jade to protect and absorb bad fortune. Jade bangles are often gifted to daughters and granddaughters as a symbol of protection and love. If the jade bangle breaks, it's a sign that the stone's protective power is working.

PAINTED BY PHILIP DE LÁSZLÓ, 1926.

THE STONE IS SAID TO HAVE A MUSICAL TONE WHEN STRUCK. CONFUCIUS IS BELIEVED TO HAVE CREATED A JADE MUSICAL INSTRUMENT.

ART DECO CARVED JADE.

In Chinese folklore, jade contains the five essential virtues of charity, modesty, courage, justice, and wisdom, and was considered the "jewel of heaven."

NINETEENTH-CENTURY EMPEROR WEARING PRAYER BEADS MADE FROM AMBER AND JADE.

ROMAN KEY RING (TOGAS DIDN'T HAVE POCKETS).

K E Y S

Meaning: AUTHORITY, STATUS, AND GOOD LUCK.

Protective power: LOCKS DANGER OUT AND KEEPS PROSPERITY IN. ALSO HAS THE POWER TO UNLOCK THE HEART.

According to the legendarium of Saint Hubert, the patron saint of huntsmen, Saint Peter presented him with a golden key that gave him power over evil. Throughout Europe, bent iron nails called Saint Hubert's keys were hung on walls of houses as a protection against rabid dogs. Until the twentieth century, if one was bitten by a dog, the "key" would be heated and applied to the wound to cure the rabies—if applied early enough, it would have "magically" cauterized the wound and potentially eradicated the virus.

In the late eighteenth century, ladies wore their keys on their chatelaines. These half charm bracelet, half Swiss Army multiuse pocketknife belt adornments were derived from the keys that medieval castle-keepers wore on their belts. Since pockets and handbags weren't yet en vogue, this was the way to keep the essentials close at hand. Housekeepers would have used chatelaines to carry the keys to the house, while an aristocratic lady would have used one to hold her watch key along with scissors, thimbles, tape measures, and notepads on her belt. By the end of the nineteenth century, a lady's chatelaine frequently held a small flask of ammonia-based smelling salts (for the fainting spells brought on by all those tight corsets).

Because the key is also thought to have the power to unlock the heart, it has been given as a love token for hundreds of years. Jane Birkin and Serge Gainsbourg had matching key necklaces that they wore throughout the 1960s. "The key was our code, to Serge and me," said Jane Birkin later.

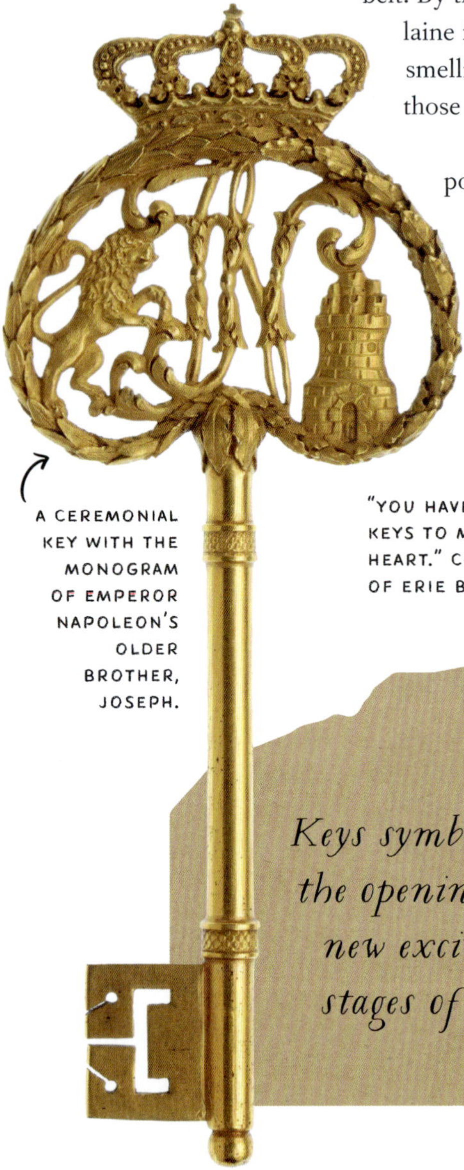

A CEREMONIAL KEY WITH THE MONOGRAM OF EMPEROR NAPOLEON'S OLDER BROTHER, JOSEPH.

"YOU HAVE THE KEYS TO MY HEART." COURTESY OF ERIE BASIN.

Keys symbolize the opening of new exciting stages of life.

FRANCES ANNE VANE-TEMPEST'S (1800–1865) ENGAGEMENT PORTRAIT. TSAR ALEXANDER I BECAME OBSESSED WITH HER AFTER SEEING THIS IMAGE.

SYMBOLIZES
SPIRITUAL
ENLIGHTENMENT.

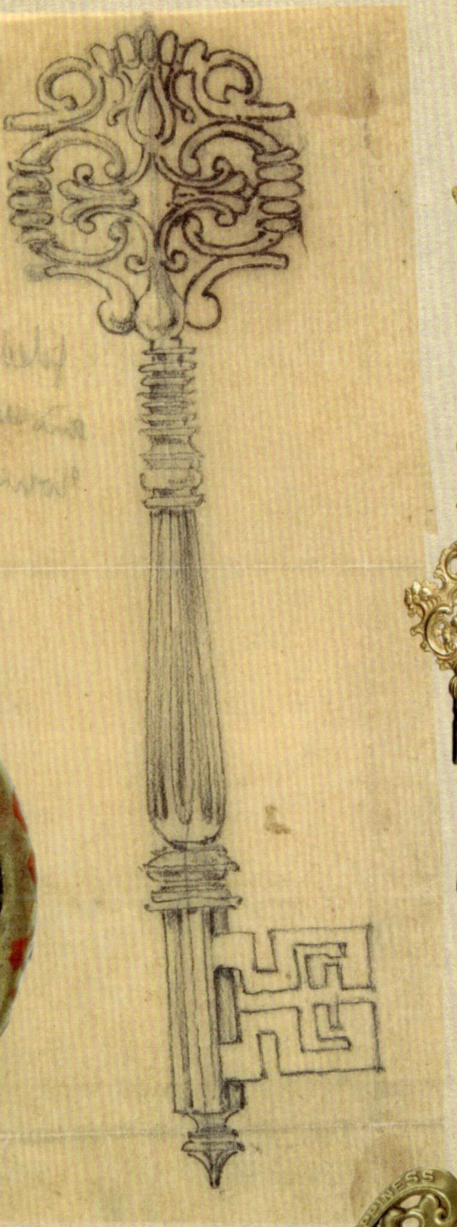

CHATELAINE
WITH WATCH AND
WATCH KEY.

ANKH = KEY OF A LIFE
ANCIENT EGYPTIAN HIEROGLYPH
REPRESENTING THE WORD FOR "LIFE."

KEY BROOCH,
CIRCA 1940.
COURTESY OF
ERIE BASIN.

LOVER'S KNOT.

KNOTS

Meaning: LOVE, FRIENDSHIP, AND AFFECTION.

Protective Power: BIND NEGATIVE ENERGY AND BRING GOOD LUCK.

HERAKLES KNOT

Also known as the reef knot, this double-knot created by two (almost) inseparable loops was used as a protective amulet in ancient Egypt. The ancient Greeks believed that Herakles used this style of knot to complete one of his Twelve Labors. His Ninth Labor was to retrieve the girdle of the Amazon queen, Hippoloyta; his knowledge of this specific knot allowed him to untie it. In ancient Greece, the Herakles knot often appeared on love rings, alluding to the untying of the bride's clothes by the bridegroom on the wedding night. The association with Herakles made the knot a powerful protective symbol. This style of knot lays flat when tied with cloth, which made it a useful way to secure bandages; and when paired with mythology's most famous divine hero, it was thought to promote healing.

HERAKLES KNOT BELT.

LOVER'S KNOT

This pretzel-shaped knot has been a symbol of love and constancy since it was first employed in Celtic rings in A.D. 500. The message of this knot is the more we are pulled apart, the tighter we become. In 1913, Queen Mary commissioned a tiara, composed of diamond lover's knots, based on the design of one that had been owned by her maternal grandmother (but had been inherited by her aunt). Known as the Cambridge Lover's Knot Tiara, it was bequeathed to her granddaughter, Queen Elizabeth II. It was a favorite of the queen's, and in 1981 she gave it as a wedding gift to Princess Diana, who wore it frequently (even though she complained it gave her headaches). It has since become a go-to of the current Princess of Wales, who has worn it on at least ten occasions, including the 2025 State Banquet at Windsor Castle for President Macron of France.

ANCIENT EGYPTIAN.

ANCIENT ROMAN BRACELET.

QUEEN ELIZABETH II (1926–2022) WEARING THE CAMBRIDGE LOVER'S KNOT TIARA IN 1953.

ANCIENT GREEK ARMBAND.

"When Queen Elizabeth I was gifted a lover's knot bracelet by one of her favorite politicians, Sir Christopher Hatton, she said that "it was the knot she most loves, and she thinks cannot be undone."

SIXTEENTH-CENTURY NECKLACE WITH INTERLINKING LOVER'S KNOTS.

THOUGHT TO HAVE BEEN MADE BY A MASTER GOLDSMITH IN THE ANCIENT CITY OF ALEXANDRIA.

ANCIENT GREEK DIADEM (THINK TIARA).

FRENCH JEWELRY DESIGN USING LAPIS LAZULI STONES, 1830.

LAPIS LAZULI

Meaning: A SYMBOL OF WISDOM, UNDERSTANDING, AND SPIRITUALITY WITH A LINK TO THE DIVINE.

Protective Power: A CHARM CAPABLE OF GRANTING A SECRET WISH.

This opaque blue stone flecked with pyrite was one of the earliest traded gemstones. It can be found in large blocks, which makes it perfect for carving. The Sumerians (who lived in modern-day Pakistan) worked it into bowls, beads, and small statues. Lapis lazuli was used throughout the ancient world for jewelry; the Romans, who associated it with the goddess Venus, even believed the stone to be an aphrodisiac. Centuries later, for Renaissance painters, ground lapis lazuli was the only blue pigment that could convey the celestial being of Christ, and it was often used to accent the robe of the Virgin Mary. For centuries, the stone could

only be found in the mountains of northern Afghanistan and was so rare that it cost more than gold.

During the Victorian era, synthetic pigments replaced lapis lazuli in painting, but it retained its divine significance in jewelry. Set in religious pieces like crosses, the stone retained its symbolic tie to the cloak of the Virgin Mary.

By the twentieth century, the gem was admired more for its physical characteristics than metaphysical ones. Cartier frequently turned out jewels with lapis lazuli accents. One gold link bracelet produced with a large lapis lazuli cylinder bead was owned by both the actress Marlene Dietrich and Wallis Simpson, the Duchess of Windsor. The Dietrich bracelet sold at Christie's in 2024 for 94,000 euros, proving that in some cases, lapis lazuli still beats the price of gold.

KING SOLOMON WAS SAID TO HAVE BEEN GIVEN A LAPIS LAZULI RING BY AN ANGEL OF THE LORD. THE RING ALLOWED HIM TO HARNESS THE SPIRITS WHO HELPED HIM BUILD HIS TEMPLE.

WIFE OF PAINTER ANTHONY VAN DYCK, 1640.

WORN AROUND AN ANCIENT EGYPTIAN WOMAN'S WAIST AS A FERTILITY AMULET.

LAPIS LAZULI CHARM ON BRACELET, 1849.

ANCIENT EGYPTIAN EARRING WITH LAPIS LAZULI BEADS.

"It is like to the color of heaven and there is within it little bodies of gold."

—ALBERTUS MAGNUS, *THE BOOK OF SECRETS*, THIRTEENTH CENTURY

QUEEN VICTORIA'S GRANDDAUGHTER PRINCESS VICTORIA (1863–1950) WEARING A LILY OF THE VALLEY LOCKET.

LILY OF THE VALLEY

Meaning: HAPPINESS AND LUCK.

Protective Power: CAN ESTABLISH A PROTECTIVE PERIMETER TO REPEL SINISTER FORCES.

On May 1, 1561, a young King Charles IX of France was given a bunch of lilies of the valley as a token of good luck. He was so charmed by the gesture that the next year, he gave them to all the women of his court, beginning the tradition of the Fête du Muguet, May Day, when gifts of lilies of the valley are given as a *porte-bonheur*, or good-luck charm.

The lily of the valley was also the favorite flower of the fashion designer Christian Dior. Deeply superstitious, Dior wore a sprig in his buttonhole at his first runway show in 1947, and after the success of that show, he never left home without one. In the 1950s, the Dior costume jewelry line frequently featured the flower. The lily of the valley is still a cornerstone motif for the brand. Seventy-five years after that first Dior show, the fashion house still sells a lily of the valley brooch for designer-approved luck.

CIRCA 1890. COURTESY OF ERIE BASIN.

ACCORDING TO LEGEND, THE FLOWER WAS ENCHANTED BY THE SONG OF THE NIGHTINGALE AND SO WOULD ONLY BLOOM WHEN THE BIRD RETURNED TO THE WOODS IN MAY. COURTESY OF INEZ STODEL.

LILY OF THE VALLEY CONVEYS "FOND RETURN OF LOVE" AND WAS USED TO MARK BIRTHDAYS, AS IN "MANY HAPPY RETURNS."

ALSO CALLED
MAY BELLS.

FIRST OF MAY, 1851; QUEEN VICTORIA WITH BABY PRINCE ARTHUR (HER SEVENTH CHILD AND THIRD SON) HOLDING LILIES OF THE VALLEY FOR MAY LUCK.

In Irish folklore, these tiny, bell-shaped flowers were believed to be the drinking cups of fairies.

VICTORIAN MOURNING BRACELETS. COURTESY OF BELL AND BIRD.

ANCIENT PERSIAN.

LION

Meaning: PROTECTION, ROYALTY, STRENGTH, WISDOM, AND COURAGE.

Protective Power: WARDS OFF CHAOS.

In the ancient world, the lion roamed nearly all corners of the globe, across Africa, southern Europe, the Middle East, and Asia. Sadly, loss of habitat has largely restricted their territory to protected parks in Africa. Ancient Egyptians believed that two lions guarded the horizons, where the sun rose and set. Belief in the lion's protective quality is why so many door knockers still bear the shape of a lion's head. Guardian lions are also an important part of Chinese culture. Worn as an amulet, the lion attracts positive energy and prosperity. Ancient Romans wore gemstones carved with the image of a lion treading on a man. These memento mori were a reminder that death can suddenly come upon each of us (an ancient way to convey a YOLO sentiment).

During the Middle Ages, the lion rampant—the animal rearing on its hind paws, as if ready to strike—became *the* heraldic emblem among European nobility. In the days before military uniforms, heraldry was a symbolic language used to identify individuals on the battlefield. A rampant lion signified bravery and valor. It was a symbolism that the Victorians could also get behind. They embraced the notion of the courageous lion, using the motif in signet rings and brooches.

Fast-forward to the twentieth century: Elvis Presley adored the lion motif. He had a custom eighteen-karat gold lion head ring made just prior to filming the 1970 documentary film *Elvis: That's the Way It Is*. What better animal for the King of Rock and Roll than the king of the jungle?

MICROMOSAIC.

ANCIENT GREEK.

ANCIENT EGYPTIAN.

DETAIL FROM THE TRIPTYCH BELOW. LADY ELIZABETH DONNE, LADY-IN-WAITING TO QUEEN ELIZABETH WOODVILLE, WEARING A LION PENDANT, THE EMBLEM OF EDWARD IV (1478).

ANCIENT GREEK.

Lion-headed fountains come from ancient Egypt as a symbol of the annual Nile flood when the sun was in the Zodiac sign Leo.

NINETEENTH-CENTURY POLISH PRINCESS ANNA ZOFIA SAPIEHA.

LOCKET

Meaning: LOVE, MEMORY, AND PERSONAL CONNECTION.

Protective Power: KEEPS LOVED ONES CLOSE TO THE HEART.

Lockets evolved from medieval reliquary jewelry, small containers created to hold fragments of bone, hair, or ashes from a martyred saint. Worn on a pendant or brooch, close to the heart, these charms protected the medieval wearer from physical and spiritual misfortune. Their power and rarity elevated them to status symbols. By the Renaissance, a locket was more likely to hold a miniature portrait than a saint's bones. The outer case was elaborately decorated and these lockets were rare and precious, designed to showcase one's familial, social, or political affiliations.

By the eighteenth century, lockets had evolved to become more of a personal memento, a physical reminder of an absent loved one. In the era before photographs, a lock of the absent loved one's hair was commonly placed inside. By the nineteenth century, mass production coupled with the advent of photography made the locket accessible to nearly every segment of the population. After the death of her beloved husband, Queen Victoria was rarely seen without her locket containing Prince Albert's photograph. Suddenly lockets designed in remembrance soared in popularity. For those Victorians with a less-than-queen-size budget, lockets could be purchased in cheaper metal alloys. After all, the desire to keep those we love close doesn't have a budgetary constraint.

MEDIEVAL LOCKET BROOCH IN THE SHAPE OF THE LETTER E.

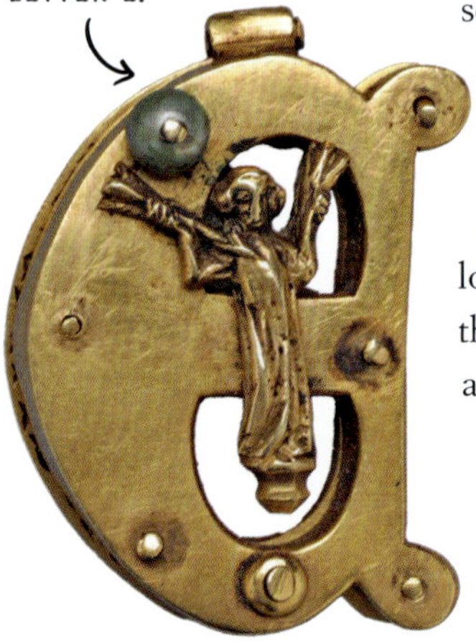

SONG SHEET FOR A NINETEENTH-CENTURY LOVE SONG.

INSTEAD OF PHOTOS, LOQUET'S LOCKET HOLDS TINY AMULETIC CHARMS.

LOCKET RING, CIRCA 1920. COURTESY OF ERIE BASIN.

NINETEENTH-CENTURY AMERICAN BABY WEARING A LOCKET.

QUEEN VICTORIA WITH HER YOUNGEST, PRINCESS BEATRICE (1857–1944).

Lockets signify that one has experienced love.

DELICATE HEART-SHAPED LOCKET, 1893.

SELF-PORTRAIT OF
EIGHTEENTH-CENTURY
ARTIST ÉLISABETH LOUISE
VIGÉE LE BRUN (1755–1842).
(SHE PAINTED MARIE
ANTOINETTE'S PORTRAIT!)

MOONSTONE

Meaning: STONE OF LOVE, BRINGS ROMANCE, PASSION, AND GOOD FORTUNE.

Protective Power: GUARDS TRAVELERS.

The Romans believed the moonstone to be solidified moonlight and thought if one looked closely, a glimpse of the moon goddess Diana could be seen within. The ancient Indians had a different view. They believed the gem came from the pupils of the eyes of the demon Vala, after he was vanquished by Vishnu. Moonstone is sacred in India, believed to allow young couples to see their future together (if they each place a stone under their tongues during a full moon). Thought to promote fertility, it was frequently gifted at weddings to ensure a large family. Another love myth claimed that if two people meet during a full moon and one is wearing a moonstone, they would fall passionately in love. During the Middle Ages, Europeans believed that gazing at the stone during the day would induce prophetic dreams that night.

During the twentieth century, moonstone's popularity has waxed and waned. During the romantic art nouveau period, it was a favorite of designers like René Lalique and Tiffany. It was popular again during the flower child era of the 1960s. Anytime fashion has taken a bohemian, romantic turn, the moonstone has become the stone of choice.

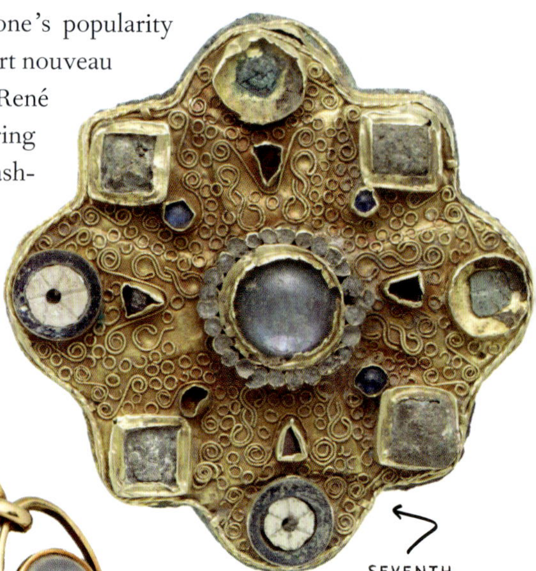

SEVENTH CENTURY.

EARLY TWENTIETH CENTURY.

MODERN MOONSTONE RING.

NINETEENTH CENTURY.

Known as the traveler's stone, the moonstone was thought to light the path of those on a journey.

MOONSTONE IS BELIEVED TO PROTECT LOVE.

CIRCA
1900.

O P A L

Meaning: PURITY AND OPTIMISM.

Protective Power: BESTOWS THE GIFT OF PROPHETIC VISIONS OR INTUITIVE POWERS.

Birthstone: OCTOBER.

The Romans called the opal "Cupid's stone," believing its iridescent color to resemble the love god's skin. They saw it as a symbol of hope and eternity. Roman generals carried the stone into battle to ensure success. All the opals in ancient Europe were mined in present-day Slovakia, which just happened to be one of the few locations never conquered by the Roman army. This meant that opals had a rarity value few other gems could match; one of the most infamous was owned by the Roman senator Nonius. The hazelnut-size stone he wore in a ring was worth about two million sesterces—enough to buy a luxurious villa in the best neighborhood in Rome. Unfortunately for Nonius, Marc Antony had a trip scheduled to meet Cleopatra, Queen of the Nile, and was on the lookout for a gift that might impress her. When Nonius refused to sell, at any price, it enraged Marc Antony to the point at which he ordered Nonius killed and all his possessions confiscated. Nonius took the stone and fled Rome.

Opal fever lasted all the way up to 1829, when Sir Walter Scott published his novel *Anne of Geierstein,* which blamed an opal amulet for the protagonist's death. Almost immediately, opal prices dropped by half. Queen Victoria tried to rehab the stone's image by giving them as gifts. When new opal deposits were discovered in Australia in 1849, interest in the iridescent stone renewed and has continued ever since.

MID-NINETEENTH CENTURY.

KNOWN AS THE RAINBOW STONE.

OPALS ON THE WRIST OF A GRAND DUCHESS. CIRCA 1841.

"OCTOBER'S CHILD IS BORN FOR WOE, AND LIFE'S VICISSITUDES MUST KNOW, BUT LAY AN OPAL ON HER BREAST, AND HOPE WILL LULL THOSE WOES TO REST."
—AUTHOR UNKNOWN

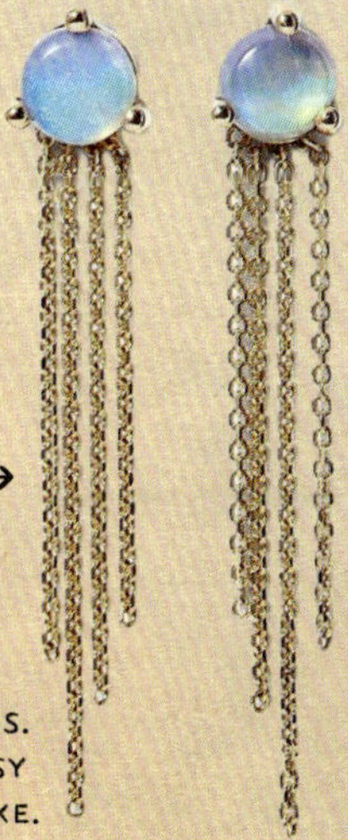

MODERN OPAL EARRINGS. COURTESY OF WWAKE.

A diamond is a brilliant stone,
To catch the world's desire;
An opal holds a fiery spark;
But a flint holds fire.

—CHRISTINA GEORGINA ROSSETTI (1830–1894)

NINETEENTH
CENTURY.

O W L

Meaning: WISDOM, INTUITION, AND THE ABILITY TO SEE THE TRUTH.

Protective Power: CAN LOOK THROUGH THE VEIL OF ILLUSION.

The owl has been associated with wisdom since ancient Greece. It was the emblem for Athena, the goddess of foresight and knowledge. The owl was said to sit on her blind side so that she could see the whole truth. It was also considered a symbol of wealth and was used as a motif on coins. The Plains Indians wore owl feathers to ward off evil spirits.

But not everyone embraced this mysterious nocturnal bird. In many cultures, the hooting of an owl was considered an ill omen. In ancient Egypt, owls were a death symbol, believed to protect spirits as they passed from one world to another.

In superstitious medieval Europe, the nocturnal habits of an owl were enough to have it branded as a witch: Some believed the owl could help a witch with her magical deeds while others thought witches transformed into the bird. Medieval folk weren't quite sure, but they avoided the creature, just in case.

Thankfully, the Victorian obsession with ornithology rescued the owl from the satanic associations of the medieval mindset. The British poet Edward Lear boosted the owl's image when he awarded the bird a title role in his popular children's poem "The Owl and the Pussy-Cat" (1867), and Arts and Crafts designers embraced the image of the owl as a symbol of both a pastoral life (given its woodland home) and wisdom (given its shrewd hunting habits).

NINETEENTH-CENTURY PATTERN FOR AN OWL STUFFY.

ARTIST VALENTINE CAMERON PRINSEP (1838–1904) IS BELIEVED TO HAVE PAINTED HIS GOOD FRIEND (AND FELLOW ARTIST) DANTE GABRIEL ROSSETTI'S WIFE, IN 1863, ONE YEAR AFTER HER DEATH. THE BARN OWL WAS CONSIDERED A SYMBOL OF DEATH IN MANY CULTURES.

NINETEENTH CENTURY.

In ancient Babylon, owl amulets were worn to protect mothers during childbirth.

EARLY TWENTIETH-CENTURY WATCH ENHANCER.

MARIE VON BERNUS (1819–1887), A FRANKFURT NOBLEWOMAN.

PADLOCK

Meaning: CAN SECURE AN UNBREAKABLE CONNECTION.

Protective Power: STRENGTH AND SECURITY.

From the seventeenth century until the twentieth, Chinese families would hang a silver padlock around a baby's neck to celebrate the child's first month of life. The padlock was thought to ward off evil and lock the child to the earth. Iranian girls wishing to attract husbands would wear a lock on a chain around their necks the evening before the Iranian New Year Festival of the Fire Dance.

During the Victorian era, a padlock pendant symbolized the locking-away of the heart's secrets or the sentiment "I have a key to your heart." The early padlock charms came with a key and symbolized love and fidelity. When a gentleman was about to leave for an extended period, he would put the bracelet on the arm of his beloved as a gift, then take the key with him (whether this seemed romantic or claustrophobic may have depended on the state of the relationship).

SIXTEENTH CENTURY.

Padlocks were often worn on the wrist as a charm hanging off the immensely popular "gate bracelets," whose hefty chains evoked the gates and fences of English country estates.

The spring padlocks we use today were patented in 1892, which made these bracelets a technological marvel as well as a romantic one. In 1883, Tiffany & Co. created a brooch in the shape of a padlock as a gift for a customer's wife. Sensing a demand, they went on to forge a padlock jewelry line that's been selling ever since.

ENGLISH EDWARDIAN-ERA BRACELET WITH A PADLOCK CLOSURE AND TWO TINY ENAMEL CHARMS OF A LADYBUG AND A FOUR-LEAF CLOVER FOR EXTRA LUCK. COURTESY OF ERIE BASIN.

In 1935, the Italian fashion designer Elsa Schiaparelli debuted padlocks on the brand's haute couture collection of handbags, as a protective seal to what Schiaparelli believed to be a woman's private world.

MEDIEVAL.

HEART-SHAPED PADLOCK BRACELET, CIRCA 1840.

FLAME DESIGN ON THE SHOULDER OF THE RING REPRESENTS THE "HEAT" OF PASSION: COUPLED WITH THE LOCK, THIS MIGHT INDICATE THE WEARER'S INTENTION TO RESIST TEMPTATION AND REMAIN FAITHFUL.

GILDED SILVER PADLOCK WITH KEY, DATE UNKNOWN.

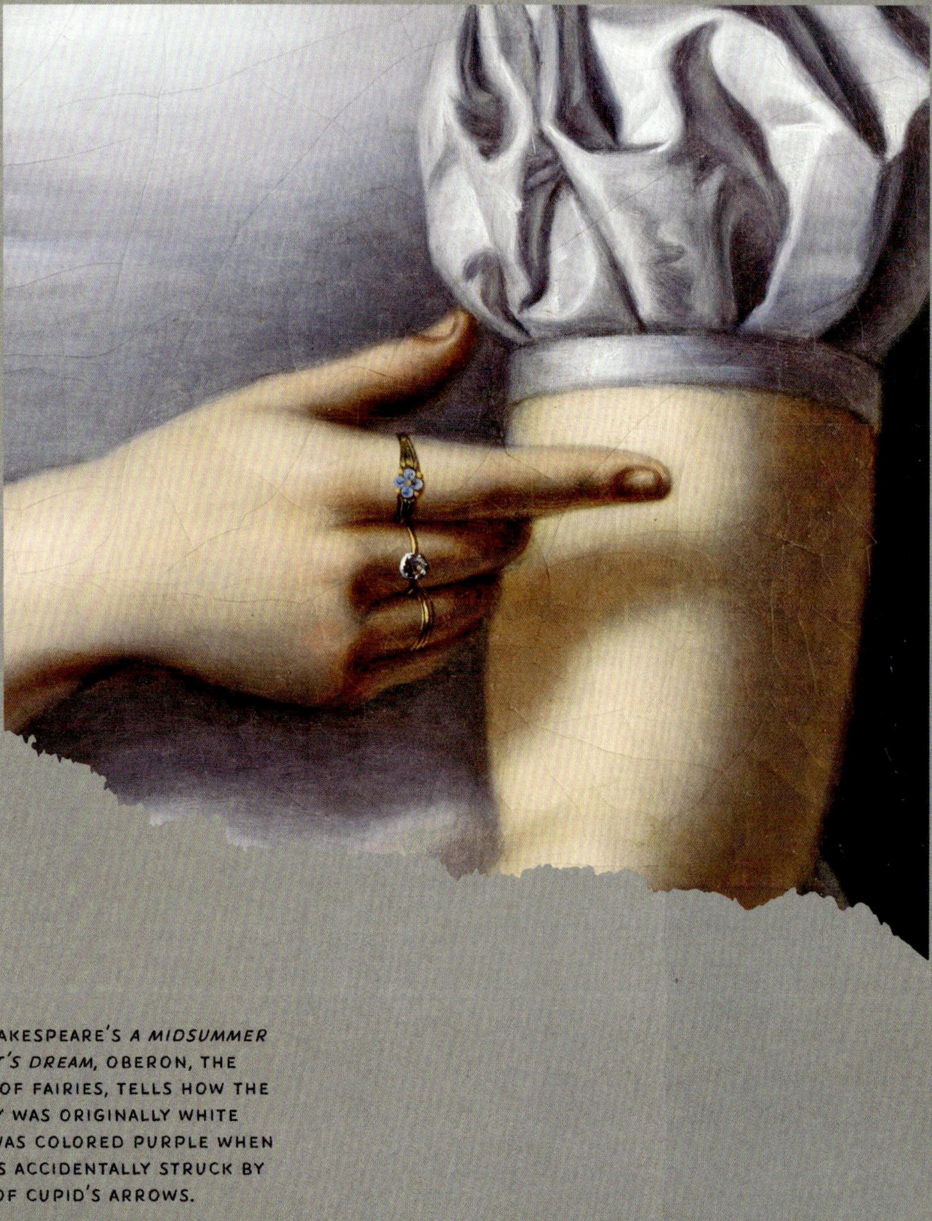

IN SHAKESPEARE'S *A MIDSUMMER NIGHT'S DREAM*, OBERON, THE KING OF FAIRIES, TELLS HOW THE PANSY WAS ORIGINALLY WHITE BUT WAS COLORED PURPLE WHEN IT WAS ACCIDENTALLY STRUCK BY ONE OF CUPID'S ARROWS.

PANSY

Meaning: THOUGHTS OF LOVE.

Protective Powers: LOVE-CHARM POWERS TO ATTRACT AND KEEP LOVE.

When *Le Langage des Fleurs,* the first dictionary to explain the meanings behind various flowers, was published in 1819, the Victorians seized upon the idea that flowers could be used to send coded messages. Jewelers, recognizing an opportunity, created jewelry based on that language of flowers. After all, what can be said in flowers can be more impactfully expressed in jewels.

The word "pansy" derives from the French verb *penser,* meaning to think, so the flower came to represent thoughtfulness and love. It was used to symbolize romantic, often unrequited, love but also platonic affection. In her later years, Clara Barton, founder of the Red Cross, was often depicted wearing an amethyst pansy brooch with a pearl center that had been given to her by her philanthropist friend Louise, Grand Duchess of Baden. It was her favorite of the many medals and trinkets she had been gifted.

CIRCA 1900.

JULIA HANKEY'S (1798–1877) ENGAGEMENT PORTRAIT.

The Knights of King Arthur's Round Table used pansies to divine the future. If the petal had four veins, one could hope; if the lines were thick and left leaning, trouble was afoot. Seven lines: constancy of love. Eight: fickleness. Nine: a change of heart. Eleven: disappointment in love.

THE PANSY WAS BELIEVED TO HAVE MAGICAL, LOVE-RELATED POWERS, AS SUGGESTED BY THE LEGEND FROM *A MIDSUMMER NIGHT'S DREAM.*

BY RENÉ LALIQUE, 1903.

FROM THE SERIES "FLORAL BEAUTIES AND LANGUAGE OF FLOWERS" FOR DUKE BRAND CIGARETTES, 1892.

PANSIES ON THE REVERSE OF A WATCH CASE, 1858.

CIRCA 1900.

DIAMOND CHOKER NECKLACE
(THE PEACOCK FEATHER IS MADE
FROM ENAMEL), CIRCA 1900.

PEACOCK

Meaning: POWER, STRENGTH, AND SELF-CONFIDENCE.

Protective Power: THE EYE-LIKE PATTERN ON THE FEATHERS CAN FEND OFF NEGATIVE ENERGY.

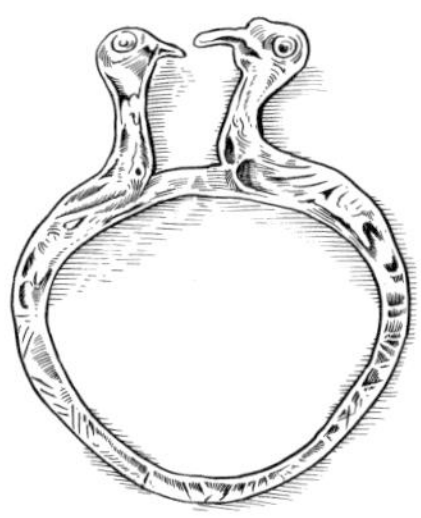

The peacock was unknown to ancient Europe until the conquests of Alexander the Great, who was so awed when he first saw this flamboyant creature in India, he forbade anyone from harming them. A symbol of eternal youth, the peacock became associated with the Greek goddess Hera and was often depicted pulling her chariot. For the Romans, it was a symbol of luxury and excess. (Despite Alexander's edict, peacock became a dining delicacy enjoyed from the time of the Romans to the Middle Ages, when the turkey edged it off the menu.) In early Christian art, the bird was depicted as a symbol of the resurrection, as its feathers were thought to represent the all-seeing God.

In its homeland of India, this majestic bird is the guardian of royalty. Considered a sacred creature, it is the only bird known to fight cobras. It is associated with the Hindu god of war, Lord Kartikeya, who is often depicted riding one. Peacocks are also seen as a symbol of beauty and grace, affiliated with Lakshmi, the goddess of wealth and prosperity.

In Chinese culture, the peacock is a herald of nobility and rank, to be owned only by emperors. The birds were also believed to have medicinal properties, and their feathers were used to ward off evil spirits. In Islamic culture, the peacock is seen as a symbol of beauty and elegance; a guardian of paradise, often featured in art and architecture.

In postwar Paris, jewelers churned out bejeweled bird brooches to represent France's freedom from Nazi Germany. Cartier made a diamond peacock brooch for Madam Robert Lazard in 1948, which perched on Uma Thurman's shoulder as she walked down the red carpet at the Met's Costume Institute Gala in 2016.

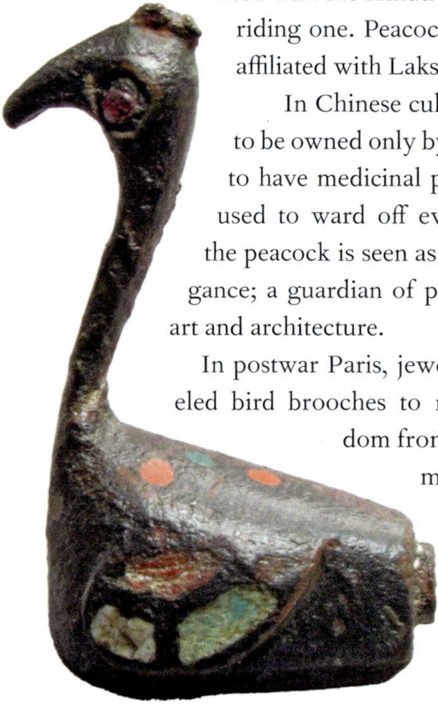

SECOND CENTURY ROMAN.

NINETEENTH CENTURY.

"The peacock has the feathers of an angel, the walk of a thief, and the voice of the devil."

—ANCIENT HINDU PROVERB DESCRIBING THE BIRD'S DUAL NATURE

PEACOCK AND DRAGON DESIGN BY WILLIAM MORRIS, 1878.

LADY CURZON (1870–1906) WAS THE ELDEST DAUGHTER OF CHICAGO'S MARSHALL FIELD, STORE FOUNDER. THE FABRIC FOR THIS "PEACOCK DRESS" WAS PURCHASED IN INDIA AND THEN SENT TO THE HOUSE OF WORTH IN PARIS TO BE TURNED INTO A GOWN.

EARLY MEDIEVAL BROOCH. IN EARLY CHRISTIAN ART, THE PEACOCK WAS A SYMBOL OF IMMORTALITY.

THE VERY FIRST EARRINGS WERE HOOPS (NO STUDS), SO TO ADD EMBELLISHMENT, A PEARL WAS TIED ON WITH A RIBBON, 1656.

P E A R L

Meaning: ASSOCIATED WITH THE MOON AND SYMBOLIC OF ENCHANTMENT.

Protective Power: PEARLS WERE THOUGHT TO BRING VITALITY TO THE WEARER. WEARING PEARLS WAS THOUGHT TO PREVENT A WOMAN FROM CRYING ON HER WEDDING DAY.

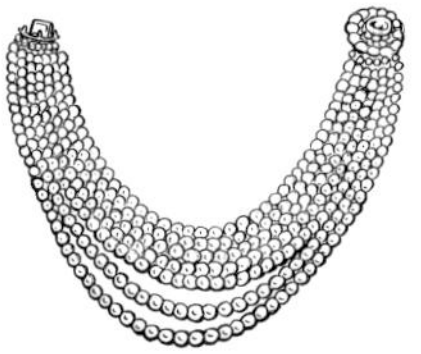

Ancient cultures throughout the world constructed pearl origin stories that centered on the divine. Chinese scholars believed pearls fell from the brain of a dragon. In Indian mythology, they were formed in celestial water droplets. Middle Eastern philosophers believed they were the tears of gods. The Byzantines spoke of pearls as miraculous remnants of the lightning bolt that penetrated the oyster's shell during creation. These myths imbued pearls with perceived supernatural powers, and early humans coveted pearls not for their monetary value but for the gem's abilities.

In one of the most legendary ancient pearl stories, Cleopatra bet Marc Antony that she could consume the value of an entire country in a single meal. After a sumptuous dinner, Marc Antony was certain he had won. The food had been opulent, but certainly not worth the value of an entire country. Then Cleopatra asked for dessert to be served, and a glass of vinegar was brought to her. She removed a pearl from one of her earrings and dropped it into the vinegar. The pearl dissolved into a slush that Cleopatra drank. That single pearl was worth 30 million sesterces (more than $14 million).

POPULAR IN ANCIENT ROME, EARRINGS OF THIS STYLE WERE KNOWN AS RATTLES BECAUSE THE PEARLS WOULD MAKE A JINGLING NOISE WHEN WORN.

In 1492, King Ferdinand and Queen Isabella of Spain commissioned Christopher Columbus to find a direct route to India—the source of spices, gems, fabrics, and pearls. Columbus, as we know, never reached India, but on his third trip to the Americas in 1498, he stumbled upon the pearl fisheries of Central America. He returned to Spain with fifty ounces of pearls. The knowledge (and exploitation) of those New World fisheries set off a pearl rush that historians now call the Pearl Age.

During the Pearl Age, pearls took on a dual meaning. They were seen as pure and godly, but the overwhelming pearl lust also made them a symbol of vanity and decadence. Add to that their erotic air from their mysterious aquatic origins and—the pearl was irresistible.

In the nineteenth century, new sources for pearls were discovered around Australia and the South Pacific. Scottish freshwater pearls, largely ignored for centuries, were rediscovered. Victorians embraced pearls, which felt less ostentatious than colored gemstones and so appealed to the British upper class for daytime wear.

They were also "allowable" in mourning: Victorians believed that pearls represented tears. Queen Victoria had been a pearl fan even prior to the death of her beloved husband, Prince Albert, who had designed pearl jewelry for her. She gave her daughters a single pearl at their births, supplying additional gems to the strand to mark each subsequent birthday. And in 1861, following the death of her husband, the queen fully embraced the tear symbolism of pearls and wore long strands for the rest of her life.

JACKIE KENNEDY'S (1929–1994) FAUX PEARLS SOLD AT AUCTION IN 1996 TO THE FRANKLIN MINT FOR $211,500. THEY WERE THEN DONATED TO THE SMITHSONIAN.

RUSSIAN NOBLEMAN ZINAIDA YUSUPOVA (1861–1939).

PLASTER MUMMY MASKS WERE A TRADITION OF FUNERARY PORTRAITURE.

STATUES LOVE PEARLS TOO. VENUS, THE GODDESS OF LOVE AND BEAUTY, WHO EMERGED FROM A SHELL, ADORNED WITH NICER EARRINGS THAN MOST ROMANS.

The gem which dims the moon.

Called "unio" in the Roman Empire because every one was unique.

THE ANCIENT ROMANS BELIEVED PEARLS WORN IN THE HAIR ATTRACTED LOVE.

CIRCA 1600.

PERIDOT

Meaning: GOOD LUCK, WEALTH, SLEEP, AND LOVE.

Protective Power: DISSOLVES MALIGNANT SPIRITS AND WARDS OFF ALL EVIL.

Birthstone: AUGUST.

The peridot is a stone created from the high temperatures of liquid magma. Rarer than diamonds or emeralds, it was favored by sultans in the Ottoman Empire. When the Crusaders brought it back to Europe, they confused it with emeralds (many of the "emeralds" used in religious objects in European churches are really peridots). Its name comes from the French derivation of the Arabic *faridat*, meaning "gemstone." The ancients called it *chrysolite*, "the gem of the sun."

For thousands of years, it was mined on an island in the Egyptian Red Sea by slaves working in horrific conditions. However, the best stones supposedly were those that simply washed up on the beach in Alexandria, Egypt. Believed to protect against the terrors of night and to break enchantments, peridot was one of Cleopatra's favorite stones.

In the early twentieth century, British suffragettes used peridot to indicate their support for the movement to grant women votes. Green (peridot), white (diamonds or moonstone), and violet (amethyst) were used as an acronym to represent "Give Women Votes!" The yellow-green of the peridot symbolized hope and new beginnings. The power of subversive jewelry and dedicated activism finally succeeded in 1920, when British women over thirty were granted the right to vote in 1918 (the right was extended to women over twenty-one in 1928).

ANCIENT GREEK INTAGLIO WITH THE HEAD OF CLEOPATRA II.

CIRCA 1900.

Found in meteorites and even on the moon and Mars.

THE SEVENTEENTH-CENTURY FRENCH ACTRESS MADEMOISELLE DUCLOS WEARING A PERIDOT BROOCH.

UK SUFFRAGETTE PENDANT, "GIVE WOMEN VOTES!" COURTESY OF BELL AND BIRD.

CIRCA 1900.

RANI BHARANI THIRUNAL LAKSHMI BAYI (1848–1901).

R U B Y

Meaning: COURAGE, LOYALTY, LOVE, AND PASSION.

Protective Power: PROTECTS AGAINST EVIL.

Birthstone: JULY.

Despite what diamond industry propagandists spin, the ruby is actually the world's most precious stone, costing more per carat than diamonds, sapphires, or emeralds. The stone was revered in ancient India, where it was said that God created rubies first, and then men to own them. According to ancient Chinese legend, rubies were self-luminescent. Legend has it that one Chinese emperor had a ruby so large, it illuminated his entire palace. The ancient Romans, who dubbed it "a flower among stones," prized the ruby above the diamond, and used it as an amulet to ward against poison, evil thoughts, and all wicked spirits. The ruby's amuletic power also attracted Medieval wearers, who believed it would guarantee wealth, wisdom, beauty, and everlasting love.

Nearly all the world's rubies originate from Myanmar (formerly Burma). According to legend, the ruby-rich city of Mogok was founded in A.D. 579 by three lost hunters who discovered a gorge filled with rubies. Unfortunately, the gorge was also filled with snakes. The intrepid tribesmen threw chunks of meat down as a distraction. The meat was picked up by birds of prey, who also inadvertently grabbed rubies that had stuck to the meat. In this way, the birds carried the rubies to their nests and were easily retrieved by the hunters. The rubies of Mogok, known for their pigeon-blood color, an intense red with a blue undertone, are still the most coveted rubies in the world, with a price to match. In 1646, the French explorer and gem hunter Jean-Baptiste Tavernier wrote of rubies, "At one carat, there is a price. At two carats the price doubles. At three carats, the price triples. At six carats, there is no price." Nearly four hundred years later, the jeweler Rolf von Bueren has said that stones above four carats are quoted like a telephone number—meaning any price can be quoted and it feels as random (and as long!). Proof that while some things change, rubies remain priceless.

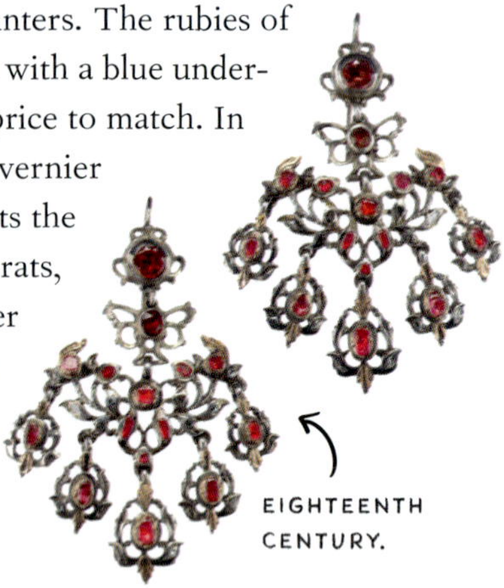

EIGHTEENTH CENTURY.

It wasn't until the eighteenth century that rubies and sapphires were discovered to be variants of the same mineral: corundum. The red version is called "ruby" while all other colors are dubbed sapphires (pink sapphire, yellow sapphire . . .).

MARGARET LAYTON; HER HUSBAND WAS A MEMBER OF THE GUARD CHARGED WITH PROTECTING THE ENGLISH CROWN JEWELS AT THE TOWER OF LONDON IN THE EARLY SEVENTEENTH CENTURY.

RUBY RING.
COURTESY OF
INEZ STODEL.

In his 1568 treatise On Goldsmithing, the Florentine sculptor Benvenuto Cellini estimated a ruby's value was eight times that of a diamond.

MAANG TIKKA,
A CULTURALLY IMPORTANT
INDIAN HEADDRESS THAT
SYMBOLIZES MARITAL UNION.

FIFTEENTH-CENTURY PAINTING,
MADONNA AND CHILD.

HEART SCARAB—
USED TO ENSURE
A POSITIVE FINAL
JUDGMENT IN THE
AFTERLIFE.

SCARAB

Meaning: CAN ENSURE REBIRTH IN THE AFTERLIFE.

Protective Power: SHIELDS FROM HARM AND BRINGS GOOD FORTUNE.

This tiny insect just might be one of the world's most powerful amulets. The ancient Egyptians were fascinated by the scarab, or dung beetle. Certainly, its shimmering opalescent shell is unexpectedly beautiful, but the Egyptians believed this tiny insect symbolized the meaning of life. The way it laboriously rolled balls of dung was reminiscent of the gods rolling the sun across the sky. And when these dung balls were dropped into the earth only to emerge as newly born beetles, it seemed that the creature itself had been reborn. To the ancients, these beetles were immortal, and *everyone* wanted a piece of that magic. So, hundreds of thousands

NINETEENTH CENTURY—MADE IN THE ANCIENT EGYPTIAN STYLE.

of stones were carved in the shape of beetles. They were inscribed with prayers or spells or just well wishes, a sort of ancient greeting card: "May your house flourish every day" and "May Ra grant you a happy New Year."

When archaeological digs during the Victorian era turned up scarab beetle charms, jewelry designers such as the Italian firm of Castellani began to design Egyptian-inspired jewelry that appealed to the fashionable set. The craze for scarabs and everything Egyptian-inspired happened again in the 1920s after the discovery of Tutankhamun's tomb, and ever since whenever ancient Egypt reappears in the public consciousness, designers are re-inspired. The scarab was a motif seen on the runway in the 2004 spring/summer collection by John Galliano for Christian Dior, it appeared again in Tory Burch's fall 2013 show, in Dries van Noten's fall/winter 2015/2016 collection, and in Chanel's pre-fall 2019 collection—maybe there is something to this whole rebirth and regeneration thing.

ISIS, THE GODDESS OF GODDESS OF MAGIC, FERTILITY, AND MOTHERHOOD, 1883.

Used in burial rituals, scarabs were placed on the heart to provide safety and guidance in the afterlife. These "heart scarabs" were often inscribed with a spell to ensure a favorable judgment.

AN EGYPTIAN FUNERARY MASK WITH A BLUE GLASS SCARAB—A SYMBOL OF RENEWAL—ON THE TOP OF THE HEAD.

EGYPTIAN WINGED SCARAB, A POWERFUL SYMBOL OF RESURRECTION AND REBIRTH.

NINETEENTH-
CENTURY
IRIDESCENT
SNAIL SHELL
NECKLACE.
CIRCA 1840.

SHELL

Meaning: NEW BEGINNINGS AND REBIRTH.

Protective Power: PROTECTS AGAINST THE EVIL EYE.

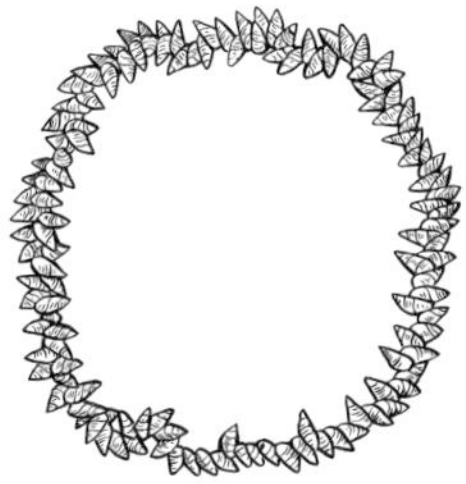

Before glass, metal, or pottery beads were invented, shells were the earliest form of jewelry. In many African and Pacific Island cultures, shells were used as currency. They have long been imbued with spiritual symbolism as well. In Greek mythology, Aphrodite, the goddess of love and beauty, was born from the sea and emerged from a seashell. In the ancient U.S. Southwest and northern Mexico, shells were used as jewelry for both ceremonial and daily wear with elaborate trade networks; the Hohokam people supplied shells to other indigenous tribes and were masters at crafting cowries into jewelry.

Along with shiploads of tea and spices, Dutch traders brought exotic shells to Europe, and shell mania soon overtook the continent. Wealthy Brits stockpiled huge quantities to build Italian-inspired grottos. The most exotic shells were set in gold and worn like precious gemstones. At one eighteenth-century Amsterdam auction, a sea snail shell species known as *Conus gloriamaris* (Glory of the Sea Cone) sold for more money than a Vermeer painting.

NATIVE AMERICAN SHELL NECKLACE, A.D. 1150–1450.

THE *TROCHIDAE* SEA SNAILS ARE KNOWN AS TOP SNAILS BECAUSE OF THE SHELL'S RESEMBLANCE TO A SPINNING TOP.

Cowries are an enduring symbol of cultural heritage and ancestral connection among Africans, who wore the shells as protective talismans and totems against slavery.

Cowrie Shells: Wealth and femininity, promotes fertility, and protects pregnant women.
Conch Shells: Power and spiritual awakening.
Scallop Shells: Travel and pilgrimage.
Puka Shells: Connection to the ocean and good luck.

ANCIENT EGYPTIAN.

IN THIS ITALIAN RENAISSANCE PORTRAIT, THE SHELLS ON THE SUBJECT'S COLLAR WERE A CODE FOR PREGNANCY (LIKE THE HIDDEN PEARL OF AN OYSTER).

PEARLIZED TROCHUS SHELL PAINTED BY THE NINETEENTH-CENTURY PRE-RAPHAELITE PAINTER EMMA SANDYS.

SOME NINETEENTH-CENTURY WOMEN TOOK THEIR LOVE OF SNAKES A STEP BEYOND THE BRACELET. THE AMERICAN HEIRESS TURNED BRITISH SOCIALITE JENNIE JEROME (MOTHER OF WINSTON CHURCHILL) REPORTEDLY HAD A SNAKE TATTOO ON HER WRIST.

SNAKES

Meaning: ETERNAL LOVE AND WISDOM.

Protective Powers: SERPENTS WERE THE BODYGUARDS OF THE ANCIENT WORLD.

Queen Victoria was only eighteen when her uncle died in 1837, and she inherited the Crown. At her first council meeting, she wore a snake bracelet, hoping to channel the wisdom of the serpent. And whatever the young, beautiful queen wore became a must-have item.

Quick to hop on the trend, Queen Victoria's daughter-in-law Princess Alexandra was rarely seen without some piece of snake jewelry. She and the rest of the aristocracy commissioned their serpent bracelets and rings from celebrated

ROMAN. IN 1939, PRINCE ALBERT PRESENTED QUEEN VICTORIA WITH AN 18-KARAT GOLD SERPENT ENGAGEMENT RING HE DESIGNED HIMSELF. SHE WAS BURIED WITH IT.

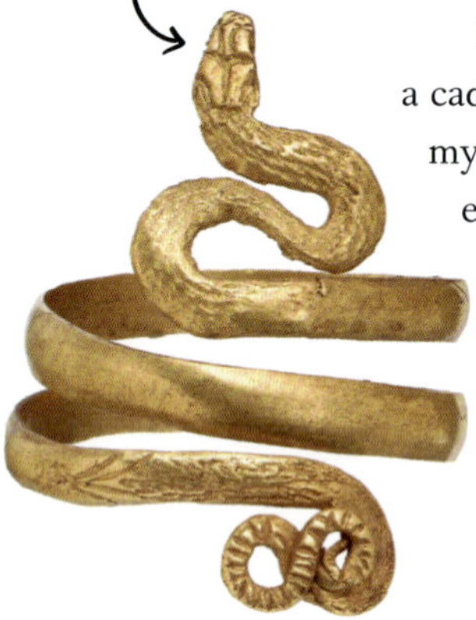

jewelers. And working-class girls could imitate the look with a simple, industrially manufactured snake ring in not-so-precious metals. In Victorian England, there was a snake jewel for everyone.

Twin Snakes—two serpents knotted or entwined—became an especially popular motif, borrowed from classical culture. The sentimental Victorians wore it to symbolize eternal love and endless devotion.

In Greek mythology, the god Hermes is often depicted holding a caduceus, a staff topped with two entwined snakes. According to myth, Hermes encountered two snakes wound around one another engaged in combat. The god separated the dueling snakes and established an accord between them; thus, the symbol of entwined snakes came to represent not only the messenger of the gods, but also peace and unity.

IN THE ANCIENT WORLD, SNAKES WERE ASSOCIATED WITH HEALING DEITIES, SUCH AS ISIS IN EGYPT.

A snake biting its own tail, known as the ouroboros, is one of the world's oldest mythological symbols. It signifies unity, eternity, and the cyclical element of nature.

BRACELETS OF RUSSIAN NOBLEWOMAN JULIA TELYAKOVSKAYA, NINETEENTH CENTURY.

Love token.

SAPPHIRE SNAKE BROOCH, LATE NINETEENTH CENTURY.

SNAKE BRACELET, 1913.

PASTE SNAKE BROOCH, 1910. COURTESY OF ERIE BASIN.

SOPHIE OF WÜRTTEMBERG, QUEEN OF THE NETHERLANDS (1818–1877).

STARS

Meaning: GUIDANCE, WISDOM, AND ENDURING LOVE.

Protective Power: A BEACON OF LIGHT IN DARKNESS.

The most recognizable Victorian star might just be one that Jackie Kennedy wore throughout her time in the White House. In the early 1960s, Jackie made frequent trips to London to visit her sister, Lee Radziwill, who lived at No. 4 Buckingham Place with her husband, Prince Stanislaw Radziwill. On one of those trips, Jackie fell head over heels for a Victorian diamond sunburst brooch in the window at Wartski, a fine antiques dealer. To afford the reportedly $100k price tag, she sold the diamond leaf brooches that Rose Kennedy had given her as a wedding gift (and had a set of replicas made so her mother-in-law wouldn't find out). The diamond starburst became a signature, and Jackie wore it to many state events during her time at the White House.

Jackie's diamond starburst brooch, in fact, dates to the Victorian obsession with all things celestial. Halley's Comet returned in 1835, and the fascination for jewelry representing the cosmos continued long after the comet disappeared. Demand only increased with the Great Comet of 1861, as well as with Jules Verne's 1865 novel *From the Earth to the Moon*, which imagined a futuristic rocket ship voyage to the moon, which meant that the solar system captivated the imagination of Victorian jewelers for nearly the entire century. When worn in mourning, star jewelry represented the deceased as guiding lights that brought the wearer guidance. Stars also appealed to the Victorian love of symbolism, representing hopes and wishes for the future. This wealth of symbolism explains why stars are so beloved to this day.

QUEEN VICTORIA'S FIRST CHILD, VICTORIA, PRINCESS ROYAL (1840–1901).

EGYPTIAN STAR BEAD; THE FIVE-POINTED STAR HIEROGLYPH, "SEBA," REPRESENTED "RISING TOWARDS THE HEAVENS." IT WAS CONSIDERED A BEACON IN THE AFTERLIFE.

JACKIE KENNEDY IN 1962.

EMPRESS ELISABETH OF AUSTRIA (1837–1898), KNOWN AS SISSI, OWNED TWENTY-SEVEN DIAMOND STARS, INSPIRED BY THE EDELWEISS FLOWER. THE STARS COULD BE WORN AS A NECKLACE, TIARA, OR BROOCHES. BUT WHEN SHE WORE THEM IN HER HAIR, AS IN THIS 1864 PORTRAIT, SHE SET OFF A CRAZE FOR DIAMOND STARS THAT SPREAD ACROSS EUROPE AND THE U.S.

CIRCA 1840s. COURTESY OF ERIE BASIN.

JACKIE KENNEDY IN 1962.

> *"I wanted to cover women in constellations. Stars! Stars of all sizes!"*
>
> —COCO CHANEL

SHOOTING STAR DIAMOND RING. COURTESY OF ERIE BASIN.

FIFTEENTH-CENTURY PILGRIM'S BADGE, WHICH WOULD HAVE BEEN WORN BY A MEDIEVAL CHRISTIAN ON A PILGRIMAGE TO A DESTINATION DEEMED HOLY BY THE CHURCH.

S U N

Meaning: LIFE, ENERGY, AND STRENGTH.

Protective Power: DIVINE POWER.

While today the phrase "sun worship" conjures an afternoon spent poolside, many ancient cultures, dependent on the vagaries of local agriculture, revered the link between life on earth and the sun. The Aztecs and Incas worshipped the sun as the supreme deity. In Greek mythology, golden Helios was believed to be an all-seeing deity, witness to life on earth. For the ancient Egyptians, the sun Ra was king of all gods. Pharaohs wore sun-themed jewelry to indicate their connection to Ra and their divine right to rule. The Roman emperor Aurelian built a temple to honor Sol Invictus (the Unconquered Sun) as the supreme god of the empire. Early biblical sun imagery piggybacked on that of Sol Invictus. (Even the birth of

Jesus was celebrated on December 25, which had previously been celebrated as the birthday of the son of Helios.)

The Native American tribe Zia uses a sun symbol with four rays. Four is a sacred number, representing the four cardinal directions, the four seasons, the four stages of life, and the four sacred obligations (a strong body, a clear mind, a pure spirit, and a devotion to the welfare of others).

In the fourteenth through seventeenth centuries in Europe, sun motifs were a popular element of royal jewelry. Most famously, when the seventeenth-century French king Louis XIV nicknamed himself the Sun King, he took the sun as his royal symbol, emblematic of his "divine right to rule" and his position at the center of the nation. He seemingly forgot the warning inherent in the myths of Icarus and Phaethon: To fly too close to the sun is to be aggressive and overconfident (this didn't end well for figures of myth or for the French royal family). During the French Revolution, the people took back the symbol to represent their collective hope, strength, and wisdom. It still carries that universal message today.

SUN ILLUSTRATION FOR A LANTERN DESIGN, CIRCA 1880.

CARTIER SUN SEAL RING, CIRCA 1960. COURTESY OF INEZ STODEL.

CIRCA NINETEENTH CENTURY.

NEAPOLITAN GIRL WEARING A SUN PENDANT, CIRCA 1876.

"Three things cannot be long hidden: the sun, the moon, and the truth."

—LAO TZU

GOLD SUN BROOCH. COURTESY OF ERIE BASIN.

EGYPTIAN
SWALLOW
AMULET,
A SACRED
SYMBOL OF
REBIRTH.

SWALLOW

Meaning: LOVE, WEALTH, AND GOOD FORTUNE.

Protective Powers: ENSURES A SAFE RETURN HOME.

The swallow has long been associated with the return of spring in the Northern Hemisphere. As such, they are birds of good luck, happiness, and hope. They are the avian embodiment of a sailor's yearning to see land again. (There is a rich history of nautical swallow tattoos.)

San Juan Capistrano hosts an annual Swallows Day parade every March to celebrate the birds' return to the Southern California town after their long-haul commute from Goya, Argentina (a 6,000-mile journey).

In the Victorian era, swallow brooches were often given to loved ones when they set out on a voyage, as a talisman of safe passage. The bird represented faithfulness and a wish for a loved one's return.

1890s. COURTESY OF ERIE BASIN.

Ancient Egyptians noted how swallows emerged from their nests on the cliffs of the Nile River at daybreak and returned at nightfall, just as souls were believed to leave their tombs at first light and return at sunset. For them, the swallow represented the coming of dawn.

CIRCA 1900. COURTESY OF INEZ STODEL.

1890s. COURTESY OF ERIE BASIN.

SWALLOW PENDANT, CIRCA 1645.

AMERICAN
KATE DEERING RIDGELY
(1857–1931).

S W A N

Meaning: PEACE, GRACE, BEAUTY, AND INNOCENCE.

Protective Power: PROVIDES THE ABILITY TO NAVIGATE CHALLENGES WITH GRACE.

The swan figures frequently in Greek mythology, where it is known as the bird of Apollo because several pulled his chariot. It is also the symbol of Aphrodite, who is often depicted riding a swan. But perhaps the most infamous mythological use of the swan is in the legend of Leda, in which Zeus assumes the form of a swan to seduce the Queen of Sparta. (Their union results in three children, including Helen of Troy.) The swan is the bird of metamorphosis, as the story of the Ugly Duckling recounts. Known to be monogamous, it also symbolizes love and loyalty.

In medieval England, several families claimed to be descendants of the legendary Swan Knight, a mysterious knight who allegedly arrived by swan-drawn boat, rescued and married a princess, and then vanished. To show their Swan Knight heritage, the noble Bohun family adopted the bird as their mascot and handed out brooches known as livery badges to their followers, emblazoned with the image of a swan. In 1459, when rumors spread that the Prince of Wales was illegitimate, his mother, Margaret of Anjou, also made him hand out swan livery badges to shore up his supporters.

DUTCH EXOTIC DANCER MATA HARI (1876–1917) IN 1910.

The story of the Swan Knight inspired the swan boats that filled Victorian parks from Boston to London. As birds who mate for life, swans appealed to a Victorian sense of romantic love. The lovestruck couples that took these swan boats for a spin might have also exchanged an abundant array of swan-themed jewelry (a tie pin for him, a pendant for her) to signal their mutual devotion.

Medieval sailors believed that the swan was able to foretell the future and thought of it as an amulet against shipwreck.

MEDIEVAL MANUSCRIPT, CIRCA 1270.

GOLD BRACELETS DECORATED WITH ENAMEL SWANS, SEVENTEENTH CENTURY.

EIGHTEENTH CENTURY.

WORN TO INDICATE ALLEGIANCE TO THE HOUSE OF LANCASTER, CIRCA 1400.

THESE TASSEL-LIKE EARRINGS WERE INITIALLY CREATED TO FESTOON ANCIENT INDIAN STATUES BUT BECAME A FAVORITE OF BOTH ROYALTY AND TEMPLE DANCERS. THEY ARE CALLED *JHUMKAS,* NAMED FOR THE HINDI WORD FOR "BELL" AS A NOD TO THE EARRINGS' SHAPE AND SOUND.

TASSEL

Meaning: POWER, PROTECTION, AND SPIRITUAL CONNECTION.

Protective Power: CAN DISTRACT THE EVIL EYE.

At its most basic, a tassel is a technique employed to keep the edges of fabric from fraying. However, in ancient Egypt, it was so much more. The ancients believed tassels (and their cousin, fringe) would protect against the evil eye because, though malevolent, the evil eye was as distractible as a kid raised on TikTok videos, and this ancient meme equivalent would attract its gaze. The noisier the tassel—some were made of metal or beads—the better for ensnaring its focus.

By the fifth and fourth centuries B.C., tassels had become a status symbol for Etruscan women who wore them hanging from their shoulders in pairs. Fast-forward to the twentieth century and the tassel was still in vogue, though the emphasis was decidedly less on spirituality and more on complementing that minimalist flapper silhouette.

This style of necklace became known as a *sautoir* (basically, French for "long necklace"), and it was almost a required accompaniment to the iconic 1920s H-line dress. If a tassel necklace seems to project hippie vibes, this is because Peace Corps workers of the 1960s often returned from their assignments abroad bearing Afghan, African, Asian, and Arabian folk tassels. And the sudden interest in Hinduism meant that objects like *japa mala* prayer beads with their prominent tassels were everywhere.

Today, tassels and fringe are experiencing a huge fashion resurgence—particularly with brands like Chloé cultivating that boho vibe. Maybe we all still need to distract that evil eye.

ANCIENT GREEK HAIRNET WITH TASSEL.

TASSEL BRACELET, 1851.

The ancient Chinese incorporated tassel details in their silk clothing: When the emperor's subjects approached him, they held their court robe embellishments in their hands to assure him that their voluminous sleeves concealed no weapons.

ANCIENT EGYPTIAN EYE-SHAPED PENDANT, ONCE INLAID WITH STONES OR GLASS, ACCENTED WITH TASSELS.

CIRCA 1870.

GOLD TASSEL NECKLACE, CIRCA 1830.

NINETEENTH CENTURY.

TOPAZ

Meaning: A MAGICAL STONE WITH BOTH MENTAL AND HEALTH BENEFITS.

Protective Power: GUARDS AGAINST LIES AND DECEIT.

Birthstone: NOVEMBER (WITH CITRINE).

In antiquity, all yellow stones were called topaz, and it was believed that all topaz was yellow. In fact, topaz can be blue, green, pink, or even colorless. But for the ancients, it was the golden, yellow hue, reminiscent of the sun, that gave the stone meaning. (Most of the other colors result from heat treatment anyway.) Ancient Greeks and Romans associated topaz with Apollo, the god of the sun. They wore it as an amulet for strength, to prevent injuries and protect travelers.

There are two schools of thought on the origin of the name. Some think it derives from *topas,* the Sanskrit word for "fire," as a nod to the stone's color. The stone was sacred in India, believed to grant wisdom and longevity to those who wore it over their hearts. South African shamans also used the gemstone in healing rituals.

The other theory is that the stone was named after the island of Topazios, whose name means "to seek," since it is usually shrouded in fog. This small, often hidden island in the Red Sea was believed to be the source of all topaz. According to the legend, those who found the island would find gemstones waiting on the shore. The ancient Greeks believed the gem could help one find lost items or (better yet) locate hidden treasure. (In fact, Topazios was the source of peridot, but it wasn't easy telling stones apart in 300 B.C.)

LATE SIXTEENTH CENTURY.

By the Middle Ages, topaz had become your all-purpose magical stone. It was thought to be particularly good at spell-breaking and calming violent emotions. Put it under your pillow to prevent nightmares. Wear it on your left arm as protection against dark magic. To cure poor eyesight, soak the stone in wine for three days and then rub it over your eyes. But its best promised power may have been to render the wearer invisible. And who among us doesn't want to disappear now and then?

CIRCA 1830.

In the thirteenth-century medieval text known as the Book of Wings, carving a falcon into topaz was said to bring the goodwill of kings.

ALIDA CHRISTINA ASSINK (1810–1886), THE PROTÉGÉE OF A RICH WIDOWER, WHO LIKELY COMMISSIONED THIS PORTRAIT TO IMPROVE HER CHANCES OF MAKING A GOOD MARRIAGE.

EARLY NINETEENTH CENTURY.

CAROLINE KRAFFT (1811–1873), DAUGHTER OF A NUREMBERG RAILWAY MERCHANT AND WIFE OF A TOBACCO FACTORY OWNER.

THE LINKED HANDS OF QUEEN VICTORIA (1819–1901) AND PRINCE ALBERT (1819–1861).

TURQUOISE

Meaning: LOVE AND FRIENDSHIP.

Protective Power: BELIEVED TO DRAW TOXINS FROM THE BODY. IT IS A SACRED STONE FOR MANY NATIVE AMERICAN TRIBES.

Birthstone: DECEMBER.

Turquoise is one of the earth's oldest gemstones. Ancient cultures around the world believed the stone bestowed health and good fortune upon its wearer. According to Apache legend, turquoise was born at the place where a rainbow touches the earth. The stone was sacred to many Native American tribes, who believed it an earth symbol capable of evoking the Great Spirit. For the Pima peoples of southern Arizona, the loss of a turquoise foretold disaster. The Navajo used the stone to bring rain. In the twelfth century, Arab writers recommended staring at turquoise early in the morning to improve one's vision.

In the thirteenth century, the stone traveled with Turkish traders on the Silk Road from the Middle East to Europe; belief in the stone's healing and protective qualities traveled with it. Turquoise allegedly turned pale when the wearer was sick, losing color when the wearer died, and then returning to its original color once in the hands of a new owner. By the Georgian era, the stone had also developed a sentimental association with love and friendship.

The Victorians adored the forget-me-not flower for the sentimentality built into its name, and turquoise was frequently set into forget-me-not patterns.

SILVER AND TURQUOISE SQUASH BLOSSOM NECKLACE BY ANNIE EAGLE, 2017.

NAVAJO WOMAN ESTZAN-NAP-PA, 1910.

THE ANCIENT EGYPTIAN WORD FOR TURQUOISE MEANT "JOY."

A turquoise given by a loving hand carries with it happiness and good fortune.

—ARABIC PROVERB

SYRIAN BRACELET, CIRCA ELEVENTH TO TWELFTH CENTURY.

COLETTE DÉSIRÉE-THÉRÈSE GODEFROY, WIFE OF A FRENCH GOVERNMENT OFFICIAL DURING THE FRENCH RESTORATION (1782–1850).

VIOLET

Meaning: INNOCENCE, FAITHFULNESS, AND EVERLASTING LOVE.

Protective Power: PROTECTS AGAINST EVIL SPIRITS AND ILLNESS.

Violets have been cultivated for their medicinal value for centuries. The flowers were a mainstay of European medieval monastery gardens, where they were used to treat headaches, insomnia, and various skin conditions. They have been a key ingredient in love potions since the time of ancient Greece, when they were also used to make a violet-flavored wine.

The Victorians got very specific about the meanings associated with each color variety: a white violet meant innocence, while a purple one symbolized that giver's loving preoccupation with the recipient. Blue violets indicated trust, devotion, and peace. Victorians went gaga for the powdery sweet scent of a violet. It was Queen Victoria's favorite flower, and she mentions the bloom 105 times in her journals. Violet pendants and brooches were popular, as they allowed violet enthusiasts to wear the flower without any temporal restraint.

Violets are frequently referenced in the poetry of Sappho, the Greek poet from the island of Lesbos, who wrote of female romantic love. In intellectual and artistic circles of 1920s Paris, wearing a violet necklace was a nod to the poet and a symbol of lesbianism by extension.

CIRCA 1930 TO 1940.

Pansies and violets are both part of Viola genus, but a pansy has four petals pointing upward and one down and more face-like markings.

By contrast, violets have two petals pointing up and one down, and are smaller and more numerous in bloom.

VIOLET GEMSTONE RING, CIRCA 1790. COURTESY OF INEZ STODEL.

ELIZABETH IVANOVNA SUVOROVA (1839–1923), WIFE OF A PROMINENT RUSSIAN ART COLLECTOR.

VIOLET FLOWER WREATH, 1865.

CIRCA 1945.

CIRCA 1980s,
TIFFANY & CO.

W H E A T

Meaning: FERTILITY, GOODWILL, AND ABUNDANCE.

Protective Powers: ATTRACTS WEALTH AND PROMOTES BALANCE.

Ears of wheat are one of the symbols of Ceres, the Roman goddess of agriculture and the harvest. (She's also where we get the word cereal). Roman wedding rings sometimes featured a wheat ear in the design, alluding to a hope for plenty. For the same reason, the bride was sprinkled with wheat—in a proto-confetti ritual.

The eighteenth-century discovery of the ancient cities of Pompeii and Herculaneum led to a classical-antiquity fever. The style goal was to look like an ancient statue of a goddess. Women adopted simple high-waisted gowns accented with jewelry—real or copied—from these archaeological sites.

For those women in the Roman-obsessed Napoleonic circle, goddess dressing became something of an art form. Princess Pauline Borghese wore a crown depicting ears of wheat as she watched her brother, Napoleon, crowned Emperor of France in 1804. And at one of her first public appearances as Empress of France, the ever-chic Joséphine Bonaparte wore a wheat ear tiara crafted from 66 carats of diamonds. Throughout her reign as empress, Joséphine frequently wore jewels with wheat motifs as bejeweled propaganda to emphasize the prosperity of the Napoleonic empire.

It was a style that translated across the Channel. At Queen Victoria's 1838 coronation, ears of wheat tiaras were worn by the eight aristocratic young women who carried her train. Queen Elizabeth II frequently wore Victoria's set of wheat-ear diamond brooches. In 2018, the queen lent them to granddaughter Princess Eugenie, who wore them as hair ornaments at her wedding reception.

CIRCA 1800.

WHEAT CHAIN; A CHAIN VARIETY MADE OF OVAL LINKS THAT ARE CONNECTED AND INTERTWINED SO THAT THE WIRE LOOKS AS IF IT HAS BEEN PLAITED.

DESIDERIA CLARY, QUEEN OF SWEDEN (1781–1860).

Gabrielle "Coco" Chanel viewed the wheat sheaf as a personal symbol of luck. In homage to its founder, the House of Chanel created a jewelry collection in 2016 called Lés Blés (the wheat) featuring wheat necklaces, rings, and earrings.

ENGLISH WHEATSHEAF EARRINGS. COURTESY OF BELL AND BIRD.

PRINCESS MARY ADELAIDE, DUCHESS OF TECK (1833–1897).

ROMAN CAMEO OF
EMPEROR TIBERIUS
(42 B.C.–A.D. 37).

WREATH

Meaning: A SYMBOL OF TRIUMPH AND VICTORY.

Protective Power: GUARDS AGAINST CURSES AND DISEASE.

According to Greek mythology, the god Apollo was deeply enamored with the nymph Daphne, who fled from his unwanted advances. She begged the river god Peneus to help her escape, and Peneus turned her into a laurel tree. From that day on, Apollo wore a wreath of laurel on his head, and as Apollo was associated with victory, so was the laurel wreath. In 27 B.C., the Roman Senate honored Emperor Caesar Augustus with a laurel and oak wreath carved in stone over his door, in recognition of his triumph over Marc Antony and Cleopatra at the battle of Actium. Roman golden laurel wreaths, first used for ceremonial occasions, soon came to indicate rank and honor.

Greek goldsmiths crafted gold wreaths to festoon the statues of gods and goddesses throughout the city. These wreaths were sculpted to resemble the plant associated with each deity. A myrtle wreath, sacred to Aphrodite, was the symbol of love and could be used at weddings and funerals. Oak, representing wisdom, was linked to Zeus. Both ivy and grape leaves were dedicated to Dionysus, infamous god of wine and revelry. They would be worn by priests and priestesses during religious processions and later given as honorific prizes to athletes and artists. These gold wreaths were the antecedent of the modern tiara.

ANCIENT GREEK.

The fall of Rome saw wreaths take on new symbolism: love. In medieval artwork, young lovers were often depicted wearing wreaths to symbolize their shared passion. Every lady was expected to receive a jeweled headpiece as part of her dowry, to be worn at her wedding. The wreath was so significant that even those who couldn't afford to buy one could rent one from a church. While many bridal customs have changed since medieval times, the bridal tiara remains an important part of many wedding ensembles.

RENÉ LALIQUE, 1903.

The word laureate (think poet laureate) comes from the Greco-Roman tradition of honoring victors with crowns of laurel leaves.

GOLD LAUREL LEAF WREATH, LATE NINETEENTH CENTURY.

NAPOLEON AS LEGITIMATE EMPEROR = GOLD LAUREL WREATH.

CIRCA 1760 TO 1770.

Acknowledgments

The image research for this book was a gargantuan task made doable in large part by Wikimedia Commons; I am so thankful for its existence that I'm now a monthly donor. Similarly, I'm grateful to many institutions, including the Metropolitan Museum of Art; the Smithsonian Institution; the Cooper Hewitt, Smithsonian Design Museum; Getty; and the Rijksmuseum for their open access to rights-free images. Without their generosity, this project would have been impossibly cost-prohibitive.

I'm grateful to the work of the Internet Archive, which allows digital access to books that were nearly impossible to obtain otherwise. Similarly, the Marin County Free Library system made it possible for me to borrow books throughout the state of California.

I am forever grateful to my beloved agent of seventeen years, Judy Linden. She spent more time than she had in shaping this project. Thank you to Ellen Scordato for pinch-hitting, and thank you to graphic designer Kimmy Hescock for turning my words into a visually stunning proposal.

To the team at Clarkson Potter: Thank you to all those working behind the scenes to put something beautiful out into the world. I'm particularly grateful to Emma Brodie for seeing the vision, believing in it, and helping to shape it. Thank you to Bri James for editorial shepherding, and to production editor Isabella Franco, managing editor Alexandra Noya, and production manager Jessica Heim. I'm grateful to Alison Kerr Miller for going beyond copyediting to fact-check the many names and dates in this project. Thank you to Brian Reedy for your beautifully detailed illustrations. And thank you to Ian Dingman: I threw you every curveball Wikimedia Commons could offer, and you knocked each page out of the park.

Thank you also to Chloe Aryeh in marketing for working to put this book into the hands of those who will enjoy it most.

After spending a decade writing about the history of the home and the objects in it, Erica Weiner had the wonderful idea to collaborate on design history articles for her magnificent antique jewelry business. I turned my attention to jewelry and haven't looked back. Around that time, I began haunting my local jewelry consignment shop, where Deanna Bartel-Hurley patiently answered every question, taught me how to use a loop, and walked the Las Vegas Antique Jewelry show with me. Nearly twenty years earlier, I spent weekends at the fabulous Erie Basin in Red Hook Brooklyn, where I spent more time browsing than buying. Thank you to Russell Whitmore for your generosity then and now, as the photos of your jewelry make this project so much richer. Leonore van der Waals of Inez Stodel in Amsterdam and Bell and Bird in Austin were equally generous in opening their digital archive to me.

I am grateful to the University of York, UK, and to my dissertation supervisors, Elizabeth Spencer, Helen Cowie, and Natasha Glaisyer, who have taught me so much about how to research and write history and who have exercised great patience while I was in the middle of this project.

Thank you to my father and mother, Robert and Susan Azzarito, who filled our home with books and our time off with travel, and who did it all on a shoestring budget with four kids.

This book is dedicated to my ninety-nine-year-old grandmother, Marilyn Azzarito, a consummate jewelry lover (her butterfly necklace is illustrated on page 51), and to my daughter, Stella, who magically started learning how to read as this book was being written. But none of it would be possible without the support of my husband, Mark Fujiwara, who is my biggest cheerleader and greatest supporter. This book is as much yours as it is mine.

Text Sources

Albersmeier, Sabine. *Bedazzled: 5,000 Years of Jewelry.* Giles, 2005.

Alun-Jones, Deborah, and John Ayton. *Charming: The Magic of Charm Jewelry.* Thames & Hudson, 2005.

Andrews, Carol. *Amulets of Ancient Egypt.* University of Texas Press, 1994.

Arthur M. Sackler Gallery (Smithsonian Institution); Lowry, Glenn D.; Nemazee, Susan. *A Jeweler's Eye: Islamic Arts of the Book from the Vever Collection.* Arthur M. Sackler Gallery, Smithsonian Institution; University of Washington Press, 1988.

Ball, Katherine M. *Animal Motifs in Asian Art: An Illustrated Guide to Their Meanings and Aesthetics.* Dover Publications, 2004.

Barnes, Simon. *The Meaning of Birds.* New York: Pegasus Books, 2018.

Bennett, David, and Daniela Mascetti. *Understanding Jewellery.* ACC Art Books, 2021.

Bernstein, Beth. *The Modern Guide to Antique Jewellery.* ACC Art Books, 2022.

Bland, Bartholomew F., and Hudson River Museum. *Strut: The Peacock and Beauty in Art.* Yonkers, NY: Hudson River Museum, 2014.

Cappellieri, Alba. *Catene: Gioielli fra storia, funzione e ornamento = Chains: Jewellery in History, Function and Ornament.* Milan: Silvana Editoriale, 2018.

Chadour-Sampson, Beatriz. *Pearls.* London: V&A Publishing, 2019.

Chadour-Sampson, Beatriz. *The Power of Love: Jewels, Romance and Eternity.* London: Unicorn Publishing Group, 2019.

Dawes, Ginny Redington, and Olivia Collings. *Georgian Jewellery: 1714–1830.* ACC Art Books, 2019.

Doniger, Wendy. *The Ring of Truth: And Other Myths of Sex and Jewelry.* Oxford University Press, 2017.

Doulton, Maria. *If Jewels Could Talk: The Legends Behind the Jewellery.* Thames & Hudson, 2017.

Fasel, Marion. *Beautiful Creatures: Jewelry Inspired by the Animal Kingdom.* New York: Rizzoli Electa, 2020.

Flower, Margaret. *Victorian Jewellery.* London: Studio Vista, 1973.

Finlay, Victoria. *Jewels: A Secret History.* Ballantine Books, 2006.

Gere, Charlotte, and Judy Rudoe. *Jewellery in the Age of Queen Victoria: A Mirror to the World.* British Museum Press, 2010.

Hardy, Joanna. *Sapphire: A Celebration of Color*, edited by Robert Violette. London: Thames & Hudson, 2022.

Hesse, Rayner W., Jr. *Jewelrymaking through History: An Encyclopedia.* Greenwood / Bloomsbury Publishing, 2007.

Holcomb, Melanie, editor. *Jewelry: The Body Transformed.* Metropolitan Museum of Art / Yale University Press, 2018.

Joyce, Kristin, and Shellei Addison. *Pearls: Ornament & Obsession.* New York: Simon & Schuster, 1993.

Kunz, George Frederick, and Charles Hugh Stevenson. *The Book of the Pearl: The History, Art, Science, and Industry of the Queen of Gems.* New York: Dover Publications, 2001. Originally published 1908.

Kunz, George E., and Ruth P. Thurston. *Pearls: A Natural History.* New York: Harry N. Abrams in association with the American Museum of Natural History, 2001.

Duval, Cynthia. *Infinite Riches: Jewelry Through the Ages.* Museum of Fine Arts, St. Petersburg, 1998.

Levine, Gilbert, and Laura L. Vookles. *The Jeweler's Eye: Nineteenth-Century Jewelry in the Collection of Nancy & Gilbert Levine.* Yonkers, NY: Hudson River Museum, 1986.

Levine, Laurie Winters. *Renaissance Jewelry in the Alsdorf Collection.* Milwaukee Art Museum, 1994.

McConnell, Sophie. *Metropolitan Jewelry.* New York: Rizzoli in association with The Metropolitan Museum of Art, 1991.

Markowitz, Yvonne J. *Artful Adornments: Jewelry from the Museum of Fine Arts, Boston*. Boston: MFA Publications, 2011.

Maurriès, Patrick, and Évelyne Possémé. *Fauna: The Art of Jewelry*. Thames & Hudson, 2017.

McConnell, Sophie. *Metropolitan Jewelry*. Metropolitan Museum of Art; Bulfinch Press, 1991.

Morgan, Diane. *From Satan's Crown to the Holy Grail: Emeralds in Myth, Magic, and History*. Westport, CT: Praeger Publishers, 2007.

Morgan, Diane. *Gemlore: Ancient Secrets and Modern Myths from the Stone Age to the Rock Age*. Westport, CT: Greenwood Press (an imprint of Bloomsbury Publishing), 2008.

Munn, Geoffrey C. *The Triumph of Love: Jewelry 1530–1930*. London: The Trustees of the Victoria and Albert Museum, 1993.

O'Donoghue, Michael, and Roger Harding. *Smithsonian Gem: A Visual Guide*. New York: DK Publishing, 2016.

Ogden, Jack. *Diamonds: An Early History of the King of Gems*. New Haven, CT: Yale University Press, 2018.

Page, Sophie, and Marina Wallace. *Spellbound: Magic, Ritual & Witchcraft*. Ashmolean Museum / ACC Art Books, 2018.

Pennick, Nigel. *The Ancestral Power of Amulets, Talismans, and Mascots: Folk Magic in Witchcraft and Religion*. Destiny Books, 2021.

Phillips, Clare. *Jewels and Jewellery*. London: Victoria and Albert Museum, 2008.

Pointon, Marcia. *Rocks, Ice and Dirty Stones: Diamond Histories*. London: Reaktion Books, 2017.

Post, Jeffrey E. *The Smithsonian National Gem Collection—Unearthed: Surprising Stories Behind the Jewels*. Abrams, 2021.

Ronnberg, Ami, and Kathleen Martin, editors. *The Book of Symbols: Reflections on Archetypal Images*. Taschen, 2010.

Rowan, Michele. *Beautiful Creatures: Jewelry Inspired by the Animal Kingdom*. Rizzoli Electa, 2020.

Scarisbrick, Diana. *Ancestral Jewels*. Deutsch, 1989.

Scarisbrick, Diana. *Diamond Jewelry: 700 Years of Glory and Glamour*. Thames & Hudson, 2019.

Scarisbrick, Diana. *Rings: Jewelry of Power, Love and Loyalty*. Thames & Hudson, 2007.

Scarisbrick, Diana. *Tiara*. New York: Rizzoli, 2000.

Scarisbrick, Diana. *The Triumph of Love: Jewelry 1530–1930*. Thames & Hudson, 1993.

Schaffer, Katharine, and Daphne Fairbairn, editors. *The Book of the Pearl: The History, Art, Science, and Industry of the Queen of Gems*. Thames & Hudson, 1998.

Tanavoli, Parviz. *Locks from Iran: Pre-Islamic to Twentieth Century*. Smithsonian Institution Traveling Exhibition Service, 1976.

Tait, Hugh. *7000 Years of Jewellery*. British Museum Press / Firefly Books, 2007.

Tennenbaum, Suzanne, and Janet Zapata. *The Jeweled Menagerie: The World of Animals in Gems*. New York: Thames & Hudson, 2001.

Thomas, Ingrid. *The Shell: A World of Decoration and Ornament*. Thames & Hudson, 2007.

Volandes, Stellene. *Jewels That Made History: 101 Stones, Myths, and Legends*. Rizzoli International, 2020.

Werness, Hope B. *Animal Symbolism in Art: A Dictionary*. Jefferson, NC: McFarland & Company, 2004.

Wilkinson, Elizabeth. *Reigning Cats and Dogs: A History of Pets at Court Since the Renaissance*. Scala Arts & Heritage Publishers, 2021.

Woolton, Carol. *Floral Jewels: From the World's Leading Designers*. Prestel, 2014.

Yalom, Marilyn. *The Amorous Heart: An Unconventional History of Love*. Basic Books, 2018.

Image Sources

INTRODUCTION

Page 6: Unknown. Countess Anna Illyesházy. circa 1840. Oil on canvas. (Image source: Wikimedia Commons)

Page 8 (top): Gold Chain with 52 Pendants. ca. 380–425 A.D. Germanic. Gold (22.3 carat) and smoky quartz. Found in Szilágysomlyó (today Şimleu Silvaniei, Romania) in 1797. Kunsthistorisches Museum, Vienna. (Image source: Google Arts & Culture)

Page 8 (bottom): Sandys, Frederick. Isolda with the Love Potion. 1870. Oil on canvas. Museo de Arte de Ponce, Puerto Rico. (Image source: Wikimedia Commons)

Page 9: Charm bracelet with silver links. 1950–1960. Silver. Rijksmuseum, Amsterdam. (Image source: Wikimedia Commons)

ACORN

Page 10: Follower of William Scrots. Portrait of Prince Edward. 16th century. Royal Collection, London. (Image source: Wikimedia Commons)

Page 12 (bottom): Boulanger de Boisfrémont, Charles. Ritratto della contessa Emilia Sommariva Seillére. 1833. Oil on canvas. Galleria d'Arte Moderna, Milan. (Image source: Wikimedia Commons)

Page 12 (top): Gold funerary wreath. 1st–2nd century CE. Gold. The Metropolitan Museum of Art, New York. (Image source: Open Access at the Met)

Page 13 (middle): Earring with acorn pendant. 1st century B.C.–1st century A.D. Gold. The Metropolitan Museum of Art, New York. (Image source: Open Access at the Met)

Page 13 (top): Victorian acorn and leaf earrings c. 1880. (Image source: Erica Weiner Jewelry, Portland, OR)

ACROSTIC

Page 14: "Dearest Brooch." England, ca. 1890. (Image source: Inez Stodel, Amsterdam)

Page 16 (top): "Gold Ring with Nine Small Stones ('Elisabeth')." Skokloster Slott Collection, Sweden. (Image source: Wikimedia Commons)

Page 16 (left): Prince Albert Edward and Princess Alexandra on their wedding day, 1863. Royal Collection Trust (Image source: Wikimedia Commons)

Page 16 (middle right): Love You Baguette Gemstone Drop Earrings. (Image source: Scribe Jewelry, Austin)

Page 16 (bottom right): Empress Joséphine's Bracelets. The Danish Royal Collections, 1806. (Image source: Kongehuset)

Page 17 (top): Erica Weiner Jewelry Acrostic Alphabet. (Image source: Erica Weiner Jewelry, Portland, OR)

Page 17 (bottom): Secret Message Acrostic Necklace. (Image source: Erica Weiner Jewelry, Portland, OR)

AMETHYST

Page 18: Herdt, Friedrich Wilhelm. Unidentified woman. 1833. Oil on canvas. (Image source: Wikimedia Commons)

Page 20 (top) and page 21 (bottom): Comb and amethyst parure. ca. 1830. Gold and amethysts. The Metropolitan Museum of Art, New York. (Image source: Open Access at the Met)

Page 20 (bottom): Pair of Earrings (part of a set). French, Paris, ca. 1830. Gold and amethysts. The Metropolitan Museum of Art, New York. (Image source: Open Access at the Met)

Page 21 (top right): Necklace (part of a set). ca. 1830. Gold and amethysts. French, Paris. The Metropolitan Museum of Art, New York. (Image source: Open Access at the Met)

Page 21 (top left): Gold and Amethyst Earrings. Roman, 1st century C.E. Gold and amethyst. The Metropolitan Museum of Art, New York. (Image source: Open Access at the Met)

ANCHOR

Page 22: Beechey, Sir William. Princess Augusta. 1797. Oil on canvas. The Royal Collection, Windsor. (Image source: Wikimedia Commons)

Page 24 (middle): Gold Anchor Ring. Circa 1970. 14-carat gold, rope-band with intertwined anchor motif. (Image source: Inez Stodel, Amsterdam)

Page 24 (right): Shark & anchor charm. (Image source: Cece Jewellery, London)

Page 25 (left): Beechey, Sir William. Princess Augusta. ca. 1802. Oil on canvas. The Royal Collection, United Kingdom. (Image source: Wikimedia Commons)

Page 25 (top right): Gold Anchor Brooch. Late 19th century. 18k rose gold and silver, set with rose-cut diamonds (approx. 0.15 ct). (Image source: Inez Stodel, Amsterdam.)

Page 25 (bottom right): Printed textile. 19th century. Cotton. The Metropolitan Museum of Art, New York. (Image source: Open Access at the Met)

Aquamarine

Page 26: Solario, Andrea. Salome with the Head of Saint John the Baptist. ca. 1507–09. Oil on wood. The Metropolitan Museum of Art, New York. (Image source: Open Access at the Met)

Page 28 (top left): Diamond and Aquamarine Earrings. Circa 1950–1970. Gold, brilliant-cut diamonds (approx. 1.24 ct), and faceted aquamarines. (Image source: Inez Stodel, Amsterdam)

Page 28 (right): Ranc, Jean. Portrait of a Lady as Pomona. 18th century. Oil on canvas. Nationalmuseum, Stockholm, Sweden. (Image source: Wikimedia Commons)

Page 28 (bottom left): Aquamarine Ring. Circa mid-20th century. Gold and aquamarine. (Image source: Inez Stodel, Amsterdam)

Page 29 (top right): Delacroix, Eugène. Portrait of a Woman in a Blue Turban. ca. 1827. Oil on canvas. Dallas Museum of Art, Dallas. (Image source: Wikimedia Commons)

Page 29 (left): Dom Pedro Aquamarine. 1992. Carved by Bernd Munsteiner. Aquamarine, 10,363 carats. Smithsonian Institution, National Museum of Natural History, Washington, D.C. (Image source: Smithsonian Open Access)

Page 29 (bottom right): A Platinum Ring with Aquamarine and Diamond. Circa mid-20th century. (Image source: Inez Stodel, Amsterdam)

Arrow

Page 30: Fabre, François-Xavier. Portrait de Madame Louis-François Bertin. 1802. Oil on canvas. Musée Fabre, Montpellier. (Image source: Wikimedia Commons)

Page 32 (top): Victorian Arrow Bracelet. Gold-filled brass. Circa 1890s. (Image source: Erie Basin, New York)

Page 32 (middle): Gold and Silver Arrow Brooch with Diamonds. French (Paris), 1885–89. 18k gold and silver, set with 114 old-cut diamonds (approx. 5.44 ct). (Image source: Inez Stodel, Amsterdam)

Page 32 (bottom): Ryūryūkyo Shinsai. Print (Hama-yumi and Buriburi-gitcho: Both Ceremonial Toys of Boys for the New Year). 19th-century. Woodblock print; ink and color on paper. The Metropolitan Museum of Art, New York. (Image source: Open Access at the Met)

Page 33 (top): Arrow Pendant. Circa 1970. 14k gold. (Image source: Erie Basin, New York)

Page 33 (bottom): Henning, Gustav Adolf. Portrait of a Lady with a Cornflower Wreath in the Background Belltower of Leipzig. 1831. Oil on canvas. (Image source: Artvee)

Bee

Page 34: Bee Pendant. Malia (Chrysolakkos necropolis), Crete; ca. 1800–1700 BCE. Gold. Archaeological Museum of Heraklion, Heraklion, Greece. (Image source: Wikimedia Commons)

Page 36 (top): Tetradrachm of Ephesos (with bee struck under Phanagōrēs). Circa 323–281 BCE. Silver. Museum of Fine Arts, Boston. (Image source: MFA Images)

Page 36 (bottom left): Belle Époque Bumblebee Brooch. French, 1900. (Image source: Bell and Bird, Austin)

Page 36 (bottom right): Gold bee locket, 18 carat with enameled bee, circa 1880, England. (Image source: Inez Stodel, Amsterdam)

Page 37 (top left): Diamond Bee Ring. Circa 1960. 18k gold and diamonds. (Image source: Erie Basin, New York)

Page 37 (top right): Sun & Bee Pendant. Circa 2024. 18 ct yellow gold, champlevé enamel, brilliant cut diamonds. (Image source: London: Cece Jewellery)

Page 37 (bottom): Gold Bees of King Childeric I. 5th century. Gold with garnet wings. Found in the royal tomb of Childeric I at Tournai (d. 481 CE). Bibliothèque nationale de France, Paris. (Image source: Wikimedia Commons)

Blue Sapphire

Page 38: Gold Earring with Pearls and Sapphire. c. 6th–7th century. Gold, sapphire, pearls. The Metropolitan Museum of Art, New York. (Image source: Open Access at the Met)

Page 40 (top): Finger Ring. British, 14th century. Gold and sapphire. The Metropolitan Museum of Art, New York. (Image source: Open Access at the Met)

Page 40 (bottom): Mielich, Hans (artist). Jewel Book of the Duchess Anna of Bavaria (Kleinodienbuch der Herzogin Anna von Bayern), fol. 87. Munich: ca. 1552–1555. Bayerische Staatsbibliothek (BSB) Cod.icon. 429. (Image source: The Library of Congress)

Page 41 (top): Bracelet. Austrian, 1830s. Gold, diamonds, sapphires. The Metropolitan Museum of Art, New York. (Image source: Open Access at the Met)

Page 41 (middle): Stirrup Ring. Late 13th–early 14th century. Gold and sapphire. The Metropolitan Museum of Art, New York. (Image source: Open Access at the Met)

Page 41 (bottom): Winterhalter, Franz Xaver. Queen Victoria. 1847. Oil on canvas. The Royal Collection, London. (Image source: Wikimedia Commons)

Bow

Page 42: Lefèbvre, Claude. Marie de Rabutin-Chantal, Marquise de Sévigné. 17th century. Oil on canvas. Musée Carnavalet, Paris. (Image source: Wikimedia Commons)

Page 44 (top): Gold Bow Brooch. Circa 1940. 14k gold. Image source: Erie Basin, New York)

Page 44 (middle): Pendant with Madonna, 19th century. Silver, gold, diamonds, garnets, and glass. Cooper Hewitt, Smithsonian Design Museum, New York. (Image source: Smithsonian Open Access)

Page 44 (bottom): Knot of Ribbon. French, 18th century. Wood and gilt. The Metropolitan Museum of Art, New York. (Image source: Open Access at the Met)

Page 45 (top left): Peake, Robert the Elder. Elizabeth Poulett. 1616. Oil on panel. Denver Art Museum, Denver. (Image source: Wikimedia Commons)

Page 45 (top right): Brooch. Probably Spanish, 18th century. Gold and diamonds. The Metropolitan Museum of Art, New York. (Image source: Open Access at the Met)

Page 45 (bottom): Brooch in the Form of a Bow (Strikbroche). 1784. Silver with diamonds. Rijksmuseum Amsterdam, Netherlands. (Image source: Wikimedia Commons)

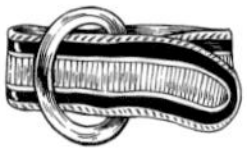

Buckle

Page 46: Kruseman, Jan Adam. Portrait of Alida Christina Assink. 1833. (Image source: Rijksmuseum, Amsterdam)

Page 48 (left): Rundell Bridge & Rundell. Garter, 1840. Gold and diamonds mounted on blue velvet. (Image source: © Royal Collection Enterprises Limited 2026 | Royal Collection Trust)

Page 48 (right): Gold Post-Medieval Finger Ring. ca. 17th century. England. (Image source: Wikimedia Commons)

Page 49 (top): Loeffler, Leopold. Female Portrait, 1851. Oil on canvas. National Museum, Kraków. (Image source: Wikimedia Commons)

Page 49 (bottom left): Victorian Buckle Bracelet. 1882. Silver. (Image source: Erie Basin, New York)

Page 49 (bottom right): Boucher, François. La Toilette of Venus. 1742. Oil on canvas. Thyssen-Bornemisza Museum. (Image source: Wikimedia Commons)

Butterfly

Page 50: Photograph of Queen Lili'uokalani in London. ca. 1887. Silver gelatin print. Hawaii State Archives. (Image source: Wikimedia Commons)

Page 52 (top): Butterfly Stick Pin Finial. ca. 1890–1910. Gold and enamel. Cooper Hewitt, Smithsonian Design Museum, New York. (Image source: Smithsonian Open Access)

Page 52 (middle): Ruby Butterfly Brooch. ca. 1900. Garnets and gold. (Image source: Erie Basin, New York)

Page 52 (bottom left): Anderson, Sophie. Take the Fair Face of Woman. 19th century. Oil on canvas. (Image source: Wikimedia Commons)

Page 52 (bottom right): Vintage enamel butterfly brooch, 1960s. (Image source: Erie Basin, New York)

Page 53 (top left): Necklace with Butterfly pendant, late 2nd–1st century BC (Hellenistic). The Walters Art Museum, Baltimore. (Image source: The Walters Art Museum Online Collection)

Page 53 (top right): Amerling, Friedrich von. Marie Freiherrin Vesque von Püttlingen, 1832. Oil on canvas. Österreichische Galerie Belvedere, Vienna. (Image source: Wikimedia Commons)

Page 53 (bottom left): Fujishima Takeji. Butterflies. 1909. (Image source: Wikimedia Commons)

Page 53 (bottom right): Hillers, John K. Moki Girls, 1879. Getty Museum. (Image source: Getty Collection Online)

Cameo

Page 54: Cameo of Hercules set in ring. Probably Italian, late 18th century. 18k gold, chalcedony cameo. The Metropolitan Museum of Art, New York. (Image source: Open Access at the Met)

Page 56 (top): Noble, Richard. Mrs John Thomas. 1858. Oil on canvas. National Gallery of Australia, Canberra. (Image source: Wikimedia Commons)

Page 56 (bottom): Fremiet (later Rude), Sophie. Portrait of a Woman. 1818. Oil on canvas. The J. Paul Getty Museum, Los Angeles. (Image source: Getty's Special Collections and Institutional Archives)

Pages 56–57 (top): Necklace (part of a set). Italian, probably Naples, ca. 1830. Gold and cameos. The Metropolitan Museum of Art, New York. (Image source: Open Access at the Met)

Page 57 (top right): Read, Katherine. British Gentlemen in Rome, ca. 1750. Yale Center for British Art, Paul Mellon Collection (Image source: Yale Center for British Art)

Page 57 (bottom): Romako, Anton. Fürstin Maria von Stackelberg. 1876. Oil on canvas. (Image source: Wikimedia Commons)

Cat

Page 58: Bacchiacca, Francesco. Portrait of a lady holding a cat, circa 1525. Oil on panel. (Image source: Wikimedia Commons)

Page 60 (top): Cuff Bracelet Decorated with Cats. 26th Dynasty (Egypt, ca. 664–525 B.C.). Gold. The Metropolitan Museum of Art, New York. (Image source: Open Access at the Met)

Page 60 (left): Perronneau, Jean-Baptiste. Magdaleine Pinceloup de la Grange, 1747. Oil on canvas. Getty Center. (Image source: Wikimedia Commons)

Page 60 (middle right): Pet Cat Brooch: French, ca. 1880. Rose-cut diamonds, ruby collar, yellow and black glass eyes. (Image source: Erie Basin, New York)

Page 60 (bottom right): Stick Pin (USA), 1890–1900. Gold, pearl, silver. Cooper Hewitt, Smithsonian Design Museum, New York. (Image source: Smithsonian Open Access)

Page 61 (top): Ring with Cat and Kittens. Ramesside/Third Intermediate Period (Egypt). Faience. The Metropolitan Museum of Art, New York. (Image source: Open Access at the Met)

Page 61 (middle): The Gayer-Anderson Cat. Late Period (ca. 664–332 B.C.). Bronze with gold ornaments. British Museum, London. (Image source: Wikimedia Commons)

Page 61 (bottom): Ring with feline's head, ca 1550–1425 B.C. Metropolitan Museum of Art, New York. (Image source: Open Access at the Met)

Citrine

Page 62: Engraved gem with Bonus Eventus. 1st century A.D. Citrine. (Image source: Getty Open Access)

Page 64 (bottom left): Guillemet, Pierre Désiré. Portrait of a Lady of the Court Playing the Tambourine. ca. 1860. Oil on canvas. Pera Museum, Istanbul. (Image source: Wikimedia Commons)

Page 64 (bottom right): Brooch. Late 19th–early 20th century. Gold and enamel with gem accents. The Walters Art Museum, Baltimore. (Image source: The Walters Art Museum Online Collection)

Pages 64–65 (top): Jolie citrine necklace, 2015. Citrine and gold. Smithsonian Institution, Washington, D.C. (Image source: Smithsonian Open Access)

Page 65 (top): Géricault, François. Portrait of Julie Duvidal de Montferrier. 1817.

Oil on canvas. Maison de Victor Hugo, Paris. (Image source: Wikimedia Commons)

Page 65 (bottom): Citrine Ring. Finnish, ca. 1930. Citrine. (Image source: Erie Basin, New York)

Clover

Page 66: Winterhalter, Franz Xaver. Empress Eugénie in Court Dress. ca. 1853. Oil on canvas. Musée national du Château de Compiègne, Compiègne, France. (Image source: Wikimedia Commons)

Page 68 (top): Diamond Clover Bracelet. 1890. Diamonds and gold. (Image source: Erie Basin, New York)

Page 68 (left): Kinney Bros, Three-Leaf Clover, Novelties Series (N228, Type 3). 1889. Paper. The Metropolitan Museum of Art, New York. (Image source: Open Access at the Met)

Page 68 (bottom right): Van Cleef & Arpels, Lucky Pendant. Circa 1950. (Image source: Inez Stodel, Amsterdam)

Page 69 (top): Lucky clover brooch, 14 carat brooch. (Image source: Inez Stodel, Amsterdam)

Page 69 (bottom left): Fancy link gold chain, 1880. (Image source: Erie Basin)

Page 69 (bottom right): Enamel clover brooch, circa 1900. (Image source: Erie Basin, New York)

Coin

Page 70: Bronzino, Agnolo. Bia di Cosimo de' Medici. c. 1542. Uffizi Gallery, Florence, Italy. (Image source: Wikimedia Commons)

Page 72 (middle): Coin. 1028 AH / 1619 CE. Gold. The Metropolitan Museum of Art, New York. (Image source: Open Access at the Met)

Pages 72–73 (top): Collar with Medallions Containing Coins of Emperors. Roman Period, ca. A.D. 225. Gold. The Metropolitan Museum of Art, New York. (Image source: Open Access at the Met)

Pages 72–73 (bottom): Girdle with Coins and Medallions. Byzantine, ca. 583. Gold settings with stamped gold coins. The Metropolitan Museum of Art, New York. (Image source: Open Access at the Met)

Page 73 (top): Szyndler, Pantaleon. Fragment of the Portrait of Matylda Godebska—Hand. 1880. National Museum in Warsaw, Warsaw, Poland. (Image source: Wikimedia Commons)

Page 73 (middle): Gold Oktadrachm of Ptolemy II Philadelphos. ca. 261–246 B.C. Gold. The Metropolitan Museum of Art, New York. (Image source: Open Access at the Met)

Crescent Moon

Page 74: Carolus-Duran. Portrait of Madame Edgard Stern. 1889. Oil on canvas. Petit Palais, Paris, France. (Image source: Wikimedia Commons)

Page 76 (top): Corcos, Vittorio Matteo. Portrait of Corinna Salmon. 1893. Oil on canvas. Private collection. (Image source: Wikimedia Commons)

Page 76 (bottom): Tiara. 19th century. Tortoiseshell and cut steel (central crescent of cut steel). Museum of Fine Arts, Boston. (Image source: MFA Images)

Page 77 (top left): Brooch in the Form of a Crescent Moon. ca. 1870–1890. Silver. (Image source: Rijksmuseum, Amsterdam)

Page 77 (top right): Lely, Peter. Portrait of Mary II Stuart as Diana. ca. 1672. Oil on canvas. Royal Collection Trust, London. (Image source: Wikimedia Commons)

Page 77 (bottom left): Necklace with Crescent-Shaped Pendant. Roman, 1st–3rd century CE. Gold. The Metropolitan Museum of Art, New York. (Image source: Open Access at the Met)

Page 77 (bottom right): Madrazo y Kuntz, Federico de. Portrait of Matilde de Aguilera y Gamboa. 1875. Oil on canvas. Museo Cerralbo, Madrid. (Image source: Wikimedia Commons)

Cross

Page 78: Portrait of an American Indian. 1900. Oil on canvas. Smithsonian American Art Museum, Washington, D.C. (Image source: Smithsonian Open Access)

Page 80 (top left): Shaw, Josephine Hartwell. Cross and necklace, 1913. Gold, sapphire and pearl. Museum of Fine Arts, Boston. (Image source: MFA Images)

Page 80 (top right): Cross Pendant. 1870. Gold and glass. Museum of Fine Arts, Boston. (Image source: MFA Images)

Page 80 (bottom left): Dagmarkorset (Dagmar Cross). 11th–12th century. Gold with enamel. Danish Royal Collection, Copenhagen. (Image source: Wikimedia Commons)

Page 80 (bottom right): Pendant and Chain. 19th century. Aquamarine set in silver. Museum of Fine Arts, Boston. (Image source: MFA Images)

Page 81 (top): Raspal, Antoine. Portrait d'Arlésienne. 19th century. Oil on canvas. Musée Grobet-Labadié, Marseille, France. (Image source: Wikimedia Commons)

Page 81 (bottom): Model Ankh. Middle Kingdom (Egypt), ca. 1981–1802 BCE. Wood. The Metropolitan Museum of Art, New York. (Image source: Open Access at the Met)

Daisy

Page 82: Rossetti, Dante Gabriel. Bocca Baciata. 1859. Oil on canvas. Museum of Fine Arts, Boston. (Image source: MFA Images)

Page 84 (top): Daisy Bead. ca. 1390–1352 B.C. Faience. The Metropolitan Museum of Art, New York. (Image source: Open Access at the Met)

Page 84 (middle left): Greenaway, Kate. Valentine, 1876. The Metropolitan Museum of Art, New York. (Image source: Open Access at the Met)

Page 84 (middle right): Brooch in the Form of a Daisy. Late 19th–early 20th century. The Netherlands. (Image source: Wikimedia Commons)

Page 84 (bottom left): Gold Love Charm. 20th century. (Image courtesy of Inez Stodel, Amsterdam)

Page 84 (bottom right): Czauczik, Jozef. Podobizeň Agnesy Okolicsányi rod. Spielenbergerovej. 1826. Oil on canvas. Slovak National Gallery, Bratislava. (Image source: Wikimedia Commons)

Page 85 (top): Rossetti, Dante Gabriel. Fair Rosamund. 1861. Oil on canvas. National Museum of Wales, Cardiff. (Image source: Wikimedia Commons)

Page 85 (bottom): Gold Daisy Locket. ca. 1900. (Image courtesy of Erie Basin, New York)

Diamond

Page 86: Bronzino, Agnolo. Eleonora of Toledo. ca. 1543. Oil on panel. National Gallery in Prague, Czech Republic. (Image source: Wikimedia Commons)

Page 88 (top left): Brooch or pendant. 19th century; possibly French. Platinum, gold back; diamonds. The Metropolitan Museum of Art, New York. (Image source: Open Access at the Met)

Page 88 (top right): Ring. ca. 1760. European (possibly made in the Netherlands or England). Gold, diamonds. The Metropolitan Museum of Art, New York. (Image source: Open Access at the Met)

Page 88 (bottom left): Raphael. Portrait of Pope Julius II. 1511. Oil on panel. National Gallery, London. (Image source: Wikimedia Commons)

Page 88 (bottom right): Workshop of Martin van Meytens. Empress Maria Theresia. 1745. Oil on canvas. (Image source: Wikimedia Commons)

Page 89 (top): French ring, second half of 19th century. Gold, silver, diamonds. The Metropolitan Museum of Art, New York. (Image source: Open Access at the Met)

Page 89 (bottom): Van der Helst, Bartholomeus. Abraham del Court and His Wife Maria de Kaersgieter. 1654. Oil on canvas. Museum Boijmans Van Beuningen, The Netherlands. (Image source: Wikimedia Commons)

Dog

Page 90: Lawrence, Sir Thomas. Lady Maria Conyngham (d. 1843). ca. 1824–25. Oil on canvas. The Metropolitan Museum of Art, New York. (Image source: Open Access at the Met)

Page 92 (top): German Shepherd Charm. ca. 1960. Gold. (Image source: Erie Basin, New York)

Page 92 (middle): Landseer, Edwin. Princess Alice asleep, watched over by Dandie, the black terrier. 1843. Royal Collection Trust. (Image source: Wikimedia Commons)

Page 92 (bottom): Brooch in the Form of a Dog. 2nd century CE. Champlevé enamel, bronze. The Metropolitan Museum of Art, New York. (Image source: Open Access at the Met)

Page 93 (top left): Drouais, François Hubert. Boy with a Black Spaniel. ca. 1767. Oil on canvas. The Metropolitan Museum of Art, New York. (Image source: Open Access at the Met)

Page 93 (top right): Attributed to Mrs. Moses B. Russell (Clarissa Peters). Baby with Rattle and Dog. 1842. Watercolor and gouache on ivory. The Metropolitan Museum of Art, New York. (Image source: Open Access at the Met)

Page 93 (bottom): Stick Pin with Hound's Head. 1870s. Gold, lapis lazuli, enamel. The Walters Art Museum, Baltimore. (Image source: The Walters Art Museum Online Collection)

Dove

Page 94: Burne-Jones, Sir Edward and Carlo II Giuliano and Arthur Giuliano. Brooch in the Form of a Dove on an Olive Branch. ca. 1895. Gold, coral, turquoise, seed pearls, ruby, red and green translucent enamel. The Metropolitan Museum of Art, New York. (Image source: Open Access at the Met)

Page 96 (top left): Gold Dove Brooch with Turquoise. c. 1820 (Georgian). 9-carat gold, pavé-set with cabochon turquoise; England. (Image source: Inez Stodel, Amsterdam)

Page 96 (top right): Pair of Earrings (part of a set). Mid-19th century. Gold and shell (Cassia rufa). Italian, probably Naples. The Metropolitan Museum of Art, New York. (Image source: Open Access at the Met)

Page 96 (bottom): Gold Earring in the Form of a Dove. 2nd century BCE. Gold. The Metropolitan Museum of Art, New York. (Image source: Open Access at the Met)

Pages 96–97 (bottom): Two Doves from a Funerary Monument. 350–300 B.C. The J. Paul Getty Museum, Los Angeles. (Image source: Getty's Special Collections and Institutional Archives)

Page 97 (top left): Pin with a Dove Finial. 525–400 B.C. The J. Paul Getty Museum, Los Angeles. (Image source: Getty's Special Collections and Institutional Archives)

Page 97 (top right): Corden, William (the Younger). Princess Maud of Wales (1869–1938). 1873. Oil on canvas. The Royal Collection, United Kingdom. (Image source: Wikimedia Commons)

Eagle

Page 98: Pair of Gold Earrings with Ganymede and the Eagle. ca. 330–300 B.C. Gold. The Metropolitan Museum of Art, New York. (Image source: Open Access at the Met)

Page 100 (top): Pergolesi, Michel Angelo. Drawing, "Ornament Design, Roman Votive, Panel with Dionysian Pattern of Grapes and Pinecones, and Eagle atop a Roman Standard." 1776. Pen and ink, brush and watercolor, gouache, over graphite on laid paper. Cooper Hewitt, Smithsonian Design Museum, New York. (Image source: Smithsonian Open Access)

Page 100 (bottom left): Jewel. 3rd century. Gold, glass-paste. The Metropolitan Museum of Art, New York. (Image source: Open Access at the Met)

Page 100 (bottom right): Prince Consort Albert (designer); Charles Augustus Du Vé (maker). Coburg Eagle Brooch. 1840. Gold, turquoise, diamonds, rubies, pearls. Museum of Fine Arts, Boston. (Image source: MFA Images)

Page 101 (top): Pendant and Necklace. Last quarter of the 19th century. Gold, enamel, rubies, diamonds, emerald. The Metropolitan Museum of Art, New York. (Image source: Open Access at the Met)

Page 101 (bottom): Eagle Stick Pin. 1870–1910. Gold, silver. The Walters Art Museum, Baltimore. (Image source: The Walters Art Museum Online Collection)

ELEPHANT

Page 102: Bichitr (attributed). Portrait of the Elephant "Alam Guman." ca. 1640. Opaque watercolor and gold on paper. The Metropolitan Museum of Art, New York. (Image source: Open Access at the Met)

Page 104 (top): Elephant Camellia Charm. Contemporary design. 18-carat gold and enamel. (Image source: Cece Jewellery, London)

Page 104 (middle right): Badge of the Order of the Elephant. 1822. Gold, enamel, diamonds, rubies. (Image source: Musée du Louvre, Paris)

Page 104 (bottom left): Denmark, 1867–95. Photograph. (Image source: The New York Public Library Digital Collections)

Page 104 (bottom right): Gold Sapphire and Bone Elephant Pendant. Cartier, London, 1975. (Image source: Inez Stodel, Amsterdam)

Page 105 (top): Portrait of Tycho Brahe. ca. 1590. Skokloster Castle, Sweden. (Image source: Wikimedia Commons)

Page 105 (bottom left): Cartier Gold Elephant Bracelet. 21st century. (Image source: Inez Stodel, Amsterdam)

Page 105 (bottom right): Pair of Earrings in the Form of Dancing Elephants. early 20th century. India. Los Angeles County Museum of Art. (Image source: Wikimedia Commons)

EMERALD

Page 106: Portrait of Maharaja Sher Singh (or perhaps Maharaja Gulab Singh). ca. 1850. Opaque watercolor on paper. (Image source: Wikimedia Commons)

Page 108 (left): Crown of the Virgin of the Immaculate Conception (known as the Crown of the Andes). ca. 1660 and 1770. Gold repoussé and emeralds. The Metropolitan Museum of Art, New York. (Image source: Open Access at the Met)

Page 108 (bottom right): Einsle, Anton. Portrait of a Lady with a Pearl Necklace. 19th century. Oil on canvas. Private collection, Austria. (Image source: Wikimedia Commons)

Pages 108–109 (top): Gold and Emerald Necklace. 1st–2nd century BCE. Gold and emeralds. The Metropolitan Museum of Art, New York. (Image source: Open Access at the Met)

Page 109 (top right): Gold Ring Set with an Emerald. ca. 330–300 BCE. Gold and emerald. The Metropolitan Museum of Art, New York. (Image source: Open Access at the Met)

Page 109 (middle, left): Madrazo y Kuntz, Federico de. María Dolores de Aldama, Marchioness of Montelo. 1855. Oil on canvas. Museo Nacional del Prado, Madrid. (Image source: Wikimedia Commons)

Page 109 (middle): François-Xavier Fabre. Lucien Bonaparte. after 1800. Napoleonic Museum (Museo Napoleonico di Roma), Rome. (Image source: Wikimedia Commons)

Page 109 (bottom left): Necklace. 1840s. Gold, emeralds, diamonds. The Metropolitan Museum of Art, New York. (Image source: Open Access at the Met)

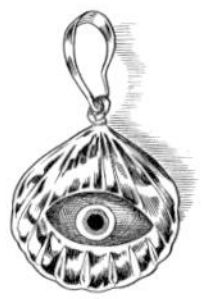

EYE

Page 110: Wedjat Eye Amulet. ca. 1070–664 B.C. Faience and aragonite. The Metropolitan Museum of Art, New York. (Image source: Open Access at the Met)

Page 112 (top): Amulet Necklace, Glass Beads Resembling Eyes, Palestine. Glass beads. Welcome Collection, London. (Image source: Wikimedia Commons)

Page 112 (left): Evil Eye Pendant. Circa 1950. 14-karat gold with blue glass eye. (Image source: Erie Basin, New York)

Page 113 (top left): Dawn Candy Ring. 18-karat yellow gold with diamonds and enamel. (Image source: Ileana Makri Jewelry, Athens)

Page 113 (bottom): String of Twelve Eye Beads. 600–200 B.C. Glass. The Metropolitan Museum of Art, New York. (Image source: Open Access at the Met)

GARNET

Page 114: Dobiaschofsky, Franz. Portrait. 1848. Oil on canvas. Location unknown. (Image source: Wikimedia Commons)

Page 116 (left): Finger Ring. 7th century. Gold with garnet cabochon. The Metropolitan Museum of Art, New York. (Image source: Open Access at the Met)

Page 116 (bottom): Simmler, Józef. Portrait of Katarzyna Jahn, artist's sister. 1849. Oil on canvas. National Museum in Warsaw, Poland. (Image source: Wikimedia Commons)

Pages 116–117 (middle): Gold, Garnet, and Agate Necklace and Earrings. 1st century B.C. Greek/Roman. The Metropolitan Museum of Art, New York. (Image source: Open Access at the Met)

Page 117 (top): Garnet Necklace. Circa mid-18th century. Almandite garnets set in silver (gilded) and gold catch. Mount Vernon, Virginia. (Image source: Special Collections and Archives—Washington Library)

Page 117 (bottom): Theus, Jeremiah. Mrs. Barnard Elliott, Jr. (Mary Elizabeth Bellinger Elliott). Circa 1766. Oil on canvas. Gibbs Museum of Art, Charleston, South Carolina. (Image source: Gibbes Museum of Art: Online Collections)

HAND (SINGLE)

Page 118: Amulet. The Netherlands. Early 19th century. Aluminium. National Museum of World Cultures. (Image source: Wikimedia Commons)

Page 120 (top): Amulet Pendant. Medieval period. Islamic world. Khalili Collection of Islamic Art. (Image source: Wikimedia Commons)

Page 120 (middle right): Figa charm necklace, circa 1980. (Image source: Erie Basin, New York)

Page 120 (bottom left): Part of a Silver Necklace Decorated with the "Hand of Fatimah." 1880–1930. Silver necklace element. Welcome Collection,

London. (Image source: Wikimedia Commons)

Page 120 (bottom right): Mano Cornuto Pendant. 19th century. Turquoise and gold. (Image source: Inez Stodel, Amsterdam)

Page 121 (top): Sorolla, Joaquín. Portrait of Luisa Martínez de Tejeda. 1907. Oil on canvas. (Image source: Artvee)

Page 121 (left): Pendant in the Form of a Hand. First half 17th century. Rock crystal with enameled gold mount and emeralds. The Metropolitan Museum of Art, New York. (Image source: Open Access at the Met)

Page 121 (middle): Pantoja de la Cruz, Juan. Portrait of Infantin Maria Anna. 1607. Oil on canvas. Kunsthistorisches Museum, Vienna, Austria. (Image source: Wikimedia Commons)

Page 121 (middle right): Hand Amulet. ca. 1332–1322 B.C. Carnelian. Brooklyn Museum, New York. (Image source: Brooklyn Museum Archives)

Page 121 (bottom): Token: black hand amulet, 18th century. (Image courtesy of Foundling Museum, London, UK)

Hands (pair)

Page 122: Ring with Cameo of Clasped Hands. 3rd century A.D. Sardonyx and gold. Museum of Fine Arts, Boston. (Image source: MFA Images)

Page 124 (middle): Posy Fede Ring from Chelmsford area, Essex. Probably early 17th century. Gold and enamel. Find in Essex, UK (Portable Antiquities Scheme). (Image source: Wikimedia Commons)

Page 124 (bottom): Claddagh Ring. 16th century (design origin). Gold. Location unknown. (Image source: Wikimedia Commons)

Pages 124–125 (top): Mourning Fede Ring. Between 1850 and 1900. Gold band with molded clasped-hands motif. Missouri History Museum. (Image source: Wikimedia Commons)

Page 125 (bottom): Bohúň, Peter Michal. Podobizeň dámy v modrom. 1854. Oil on canvas. East Slovak Gallery, Košice, Slovakia. (Image source: Wikimedia Commons)

Heart

Page 126: Cranach, Lucas I. Portrait de Sibylle de Clève, électrice de Saxe. 1531. Oil on panel. Fondation Bemberg, Toulouse. (Image source: Wikimedia Commons)

Page 128 (left): Flemish Heart Pendant. Circa 1785–1800. Silver and diamonds. (Image source: Rijksmuseum, Amsterdam)

Page 128 (right): Rossetti, Dante Gabriel. A Vision of Fiammetta. 1878. Oil on panel. Andrew Lloyd Webber Collection. (Image source: Wikimedia Commons)

Page 129 (top left): Krafft, Barbara. Porträt Anna Maria Lergetporer. 1811. Oil on canvas. (Image source: Wikimedia Commons)

Page 129 (top right): Ring with lady with the unicorn. C. 1550–1600. Gold, enamel, and diamond ring. (Image source: Rijksmuseum, Amsterdam)

Page 129 (bottom): Vallain, Nanine. Portrait of a Lady. c. 1805. Oil on canvas. National Gallery of Ireland, Dublin. (Image source: Wikimedia Commons)

Horseshoe

Page 130: Sarony, Napoleon. John Drew, Jr. 1875. Albumen silver print. The J. Paul Getty Museum, Los Angeles. (Image source: Getty's Special Collections and Institutional Archives)

Page 132 (top): Diamond Horseshoe Ring. Circa 1900. Gold and diamonds. (Image source: Erie Basin, New York)

Page 132 (bottom left): Victorian era horse hoof locket. (Image source: Bell and Bird, Austin)

Page 132 (bottom right): Hancock, Charles. Lady Portarlington on a Grey Horse. 1845. Oil on canvas. National Trust, Mount Stewart, Northern Ireland. (Image source: Wikimedia Commons)

Page 133 (top): Diamond horseshoe bracelet. (Image source: Bell and Bird, Austin)

Page 133 (middle left): Kiørboe, Carl Friederich. Empress Eugénie on Horseback. Between 1853–1876. Oil on canvas. Statens Museum for Kunst, Copenhagen. (Image source: Wikimedia Commons)

Page 133 (right): Victorian era ruby horseshoe pendant. (Image source: Bell and Bird, Austin)

Page 133 (bottom): Pearl Horseshoe Bracelet. Circa 1890. Gold and pearls. (Image source: Erie Basin, New York)

Hummingbird

Page 134: Earrings. Circa 1865. Preserved hummingbird, gold, and metal. The Metropolitan Museum of Art, New York. (Image source: Open Access at the Met)

Page 136 (top): Van Cleef & Arpels. Hummingbird Brooch. 20th century. Gold and gems. (Image source: Inez Stodel, Amsterdam)

Page 136 (bottom): Haeckel, Ernst. Trochilidae (Hummingbirds). 1904. Color lithograph from Kunstformen der Natur (Art Forms in Nature). Leipzig: Bibliographisches Institut. (Image source: Wikimedia Commons)

Page 137 (top): Hummingbird from The Birds of America from Drawings Made in the United States. 1888. Hand-colored lithograph. The Metropolitan Museum of Art, New York. (Image source: Open Access at the Met)

Page 137 (bottom): Diamond Hummingbird Brooch. 20th century. Gold and diamonds. (Image source: Erie Basin, New York)

Jade

Page 138: de László, Philip Alexius. Winnie Melville, Mrs Derek Oldham. 1920. Oil on canvas. Private collection. (Image source: Wikimedia Commons)

Page 140 (bottom left): de László, Philip Alexius. Portrait of a Lady. 1926. Oil on canvas. Private collection. (Image source: Wikimedia Commons)

Page 140 (bottom middle): Jade Bangle with Gem-Set Decoration. Circa 1950. Gold, sapphire, ruby, jade, and opal. Museum of Fine Arts, Boston. (Image source: MFA Images)

Pages 140–141 (top): 't Hart, Frederik. White Gold Bracelet with Jade and Diamonds. Circa 1924–1934. White gold, jade, and diamonds. (Image source: Rijksmuseum, Amsterdam)

Pages 140–141 (bottom): Siberian Nephrite Jade Bangle. Nephrite jade. Kim Qui Gems, Hanoi, Vietnam. (Image source: Wikimedia Commons)

Page 141 (right): Portrait of Qianlong Emperor As a Young Man. 19th century. Hanging scroll; ink and color on silk. The Metropolitan Museum of Art, New York. (Image source: Open Access at the Met)

Keys

Page 142: Roman Key Ring with Inscription. 4th century. Gold. The Metropolitan Museum of Art, New York. (Image source: Open Access at the Met)

Page 144 (left): French. Key. ca. 1808–13. Gilt bronze. The Metropolitan Museum of Art, New York. (Image source: Open Access at the Met)

Page 144 (right): Key to My Heart Charm. Circa 1950. Gold and gem-set. (Image source: Erie Basin, New York)

Page 144 (bottom): Lawrence, Sir Thomas. Portrait of Frances Anne Emily Vane-Tempest, later Marchioness of Londonderry. 1818. Oil on canvas. National Trust, Mount Stewart, County Down. (Image source: Wikimedia Commons)

Page 145 (left): Cowroid Inscribed with an Ankh. ca. 1492–1473 B.C. Hematite and gold. The Metropolitan Museum of Art, New York. (Image source: Open Access at the Met)

Page 145 (middle): Key. second half 19th century. Graphite on tracing paper. The Metropolitan Museum of Art, New York. (Image source: Open Access at the Met)

Page 145 (right): Chatelaine with Watch. 18th century. Gold, gilt metal, agate, and rock crystal. The Walters Art Museum, Baltimore. (Image source: The Walters Art Museum Online Collection)

Page 145 (bottom right): Vintage Key to Happiness brooch. (Image source: Erie Basin, New York)

Knots

Page 146: Einsle, Anton. Therese Edle v. Mannagetta geb. Edle v. Schickh. 1841. Oil on canvas. (Image source: Wikimedia Commons)

Page 148 (top): Deckler, Carl Friedrich. Vestal with Ivy Garland. 1856. Oil on canvas. (Image source: Wikimedia Commons)

Page 148 (bottom left): Reef Knot Bracelet. 2130–1980 B.C. Gold. Museum of Fine Arts, Boston. (Image source: MFA Images)

Page 148 (bottom right): Bracelet with spirally twisted strands and a Herakles knot at the bezel. A.D. 2nd century. Gold. The Metropolitan Museum of Art, New York. (Image source: Open Access at the Met)

Page 148–149 (middle): Necklace with interlinking lovers knots. England, 1590–1620. Gold with white enamel. Victoria and Albert Museum, London. (Image source: Wikimedia Commons)

Page 149 (top left): Queen Elizabeth II and Geoffrey Tremaine Mayor of Palmerston North. January 1954. Photograph. (Image source: Wikimedia Commons)

Page 149 (top right): Gold armband with Herakles knot. 3rd–2nd century B.C. Gold inlaid with garnets, emeralds, and enamel. The Metropolitan Museum of Art, New York. (Image source: Open Access at the Met)

Page 149 (middle): Diadem. Circa 225–175 B.C. Gold, glass paste, bone or pearl, garnet, cornelian and moonstone. The J. Paul Getty Museum, Los Angeles. (Image source: Getty's Special Collections and Institutional Archives)

Page 149 (bottom): Gold cross-strap diadem with a Herakles knot set with five garnets. ca. 300–250 B.C. Gold and garnet. The Metropolitan Museum of Art, New York. (Image source: Open Access at the Met)

Lapis Lazuli

Page 150: Falize, Alexis. Drawing of a costume accessory (Parure of diadem, brooch, and necklace with lapis lazuli and enamel). ca. 1830–70. Graphite, pen and black ink, watercolor and gouache on brown paper. The Metropolitan Museum of Art, New York. (Image source: Open Access at the Met)

Page 152 (left): Scarab Ring of Shoshenq III. 823–772 B.C. Gold and lapis lazuli. Museum of Fine Arts, Boston. (Image source: MFA Images)

Page 152 (bottom): van Dyck, Anthony. Mary Ruthven, Lady van Dyck. 1640. Oil on canvas. Museo Nacional del Prado, Madrid. (Image source: Wikimedia Commons)

Pages 152–153 (top): Girdle with gold and lapis wallet-shaped beads. ca. 1479–1425 B.C. Gold and lapis lazuli. The Metropolitan Museum of Art, New York. (Image source: Open Access at the Met)

Page 153 (right): Dubufe, Édouard Louis. Anne-Arsène Charton (1827–1892). 1849. Oil on canvas. Private collection. (Image source: Wikimedia Commons)

Page 153 (bottom): Beaded Penannular Earring. ca. 1991–1450 B.C. Gold and lapis lazuli. The Metropolitan Museum of Art, New York. (Image source: Open Access at the Met)

Lily of the Valley

Page 154: Koberwein, George. Princess Victoria of Wales. 1870s. Oil on canvas. Royal Collection, United Kingdom. (Image source: Wikimedia Commons)

Page 156 (top): Lily of the Valley locket. 1890. Enamel and yellow gold. (Image source: Erie Basin, New York)

Page 156 (left): Gold Locket with Enamel and Pearls (Necklace Pendant). Victorian. Gold, enamel, pearls. (Image source: Ines Stodel, Amsterdam)

Page 156 (bottom): Guillemet, Pierre Désiré. Portrait of a Lady of the Court Playing the Tambourine. 1875 Oil on canvas. Pera Museum, Turkey. (Image source: Wikimedia Commons)

Page 157 (top): Winterhalter, Franz Xaver. May Day. 1851. Oil on canvas. Royal Collection, United Kingdom. (Image source: Wikimedia Commons)

Page 157 (left): Lily of the Valley (Convallaria Majalis), from the Flowers series for Old Judge Cigarettes. 1890. Commercial color lithograph. The Metropolitan Museum of Art, New York. (Image source: Open Access at the Met)

Page 157 (bottom right): Victorian era black enamel bangle set. (Image source: Bell and Bird, Austin)

Lion

Page 158: Appliqué in the Shape of a Lion's Head. Circa 6th–4th century B.C. Gold. The Metropolitan Museum of Art, New York. (Image source: Open Access at the Met)

Page 160 (left): Box with Lion, and a Dog and Duck. 1825–1850. Gold and glass tesserae (micromosaic). The Walters Art Museum, Baltimore. (Image source: The Walters Art Museum Online Collection)

Page 160 (middle right): Gold Lion-Head Pendant. Second half of the 5th century B.C. Gold. The Metropolitan Museum of Art, New York. (Image source: Open Access at the Met)

Pages 160–161 (middle): Memling, Hans. The Donne Triptych. Circa 1478. Oil on oak panel. National Gallery, London. (Image source: Wikimedia Commons)

Pages 160–161 (bottom): Lion Bracelet of Sithathoryunet. Circa 1887–1813 B.C. Gold and amethyst. The Metropolitan Museum of Art, New York. (Image source: Open Access at the Met)

Page 161 (bottom): Silver Bracelet with Gold Lion's Head Finials. 5th–4th century B.C. Silver and gold. The Metropolitan Museum of Art, New York. (Image source: Open Access at the Met)

Locket

Page 162: Portrait of Anna Sapieha. 1820. Oil on cardboard. National Museum in Warsaw, Poland. (Image source: NMW Archives)

Page 164 (top left): Amatory Brooch. Circa 1340–1360. Gold and freshwater pearl. The Metropolitan Museum of Art, New York. (Image source: Open Access at the Met)

Page 164 (middle left): Jupiter Gold Locket. (Image source: Loquet. London, United Kingdom)

Page 164 (right): Keen, Walter P. You, Only You. 1895. Sheet music; words and music by Walter P. Keen, cover illustration by J. E. Rosenthal. (Image source: New York Public Library, American Popular Songs Collection)

Page 165 (top left): American 19th Century. Baby with Locket. 1813. Oil on canvas. National Gallery of Art, Washington, D.C. (Image source: Wikimedia Commons)

Page 165 (top right): Princess Beatrice of Battenberg and Queen Victoria. 1905. Photograph. National Portrait Gallery, United Kingdom. (Image source: Wikimedia Commons)

Page 165 (bottom): Ebert, Anton. Porträt einer Dame in blauem Kleid. 1893. Oil on canvas. Location unknown. (Image source: Wikimedia Commons)

Moonstone

Page 166: Vigée Le Brun, Élisabeth. Self-Portrait. 1781–82. Oil on canvas. Kimbell Art Museum, Fort Worth, Texas. (Image source: Wikimedia Commons)

Page 168 (top right): Disk Brooch. Second half of 7th century. Gold sheet, filigree, moonstone/adularia, glass cabochons. The Metropolitan Museum of Art, New York. (Image source: Open Access at the Met)

Page 168 (left): Bracelet with four moonstones. Circa early 20th century. Gold and four moonstones. (Image source: Rijksmuseum, Amsterdam)

Page 168 (bottom right): Bezel-set Moonstone Ring in Yellow Gold. Circa early 20th century. Yellow gold and moonstone. CG Jewelry. (Image source: Wikimedia Commons)

Page 169 (left): Earrings. 19th century. Moonstone with gilt metal. Museum of Fine Arts, Boston. (Image source: MFA Images)

Page 169 (right): Feuerbach, Anselm. Portrait of Nanna Risi. 1861. Oil on canvas. Staatliche Kunsthalle Karlsruhe (formerly Grand Ducal Gallery), Karlsruhe. (Image source: Staatliche Kunsthalle Karlsruhe archives)

Opal

Page 170: Marcus & Co. Brooch. Circa 1900. Gold, opal, and enamel. The Metropolitan Museum of Art, New York. (Image source: Open Access at the Met)

Page 172 (left): Earrings. 19th century. Moonstone with gilt metal. Museum of Fine Arts, Boston. (Image source: MFA Images)

Page 172 (right): Schlesinger, Henri Guillaume. Portrait of Madame Valérie Schayé (1817–1906). 1843. Oil on canvas. Musée du Louvre, Paris. (Image source: Louvre Site des Collections)

Page 173 (top left): Schiavoni, Felice. Portrait of Grand Duchess Elena Paulowna. 1838. Oil on canvas. Gallerie dell'Accademia, Venice. (Image source: Wikimedia Commons)

Page 173 (right): Popp, Mișu. Portret de femeie. Second half of the 19th century. Oil on canvas. National Museum of Art of the Republic of Moldova, Chişinău. (Image source: Wikimedia Commons)

Page 173 (bottom left): Haze Earrings. Contemporary (2020s). 14k solid recycled yellow gold and 4 mm Australian opal. (Image source: WWAKE, New York)

Owl

Page 174: Firm of Castellani. Brooch in the Form of an Owl Head. ca. 1860. Gold and agate. The Metropolitan Museum of Art, New York. (Image source: Open Access at the Met)

Page 176: Textile, The Owl. 1892. Cotton printed panel. Cooper Hewitt, Smithsonian Design Museum, New York. (Image source: Smithsonian Open Access)

Page 177 (top left): Prinsep, Valentine Cameron. Il Barbagianni (The Owl). 1863. Oil on canvas. (Image source: Wikimedia Commons)

Page 177 (right): Owl Pendant. ca. 1900. Gold and enamel. The Walters Art Museum, Baltimore. (Image source: The Walters Art Museum Online Collection)

Page 177 (bottom): Tiffany & Co. Owl Watch Enhancer with Outstretched Wings. ca. 1900. Gold, enamel, and glass. Museum of Fine Arts, Boston. (Image source: MFA Images)

Padlock

Page 178: Veit, Philipp. Portrait of the Baroness of Bernus. 1838. Oil on canvas. Städel Museum, Frankfurt am Main. (Image source: Wikimedia Commons)

Page 180 (left): Gold Padlock Bracelet. 1904. Gold. (Image source: Erie Basin, New York)

Page 180 (right): Omereler, André. Steel with partially gilded brass padlock and key, 1531. Metropolitan Museum of Art. (Image source: Open Access at the Met)

Page 180 (bottom): Padlock locket. ca. 1450–1500. (Image source: Wikimedia Commons)

Page 181 (top): Winterhalter, Franz Xaver. Marie-Thécle de Monttessuy, Comtesse de Nieuwerkerke. 1840. Oil on canvas. Landesmuseum Mainz, Germany. (Image source: Wikimedia Commons)

Page 181 (right): Medieval Gold "Fidelity in Love" Lock Ring. ca. 1400–1500. Gold. (Image source: Wikimedia Commons)

Page 181 (bottom left): Padlock of Gilded Silver with Key. Date unknown. Gilded silver. (Image source: Rijksmuseum, Amsterdam)

Pansy

Page 182: Herrmann, Johann. Portrait eines jungen Mädchens mit Kranz und Perlenkette. 1823. Oil on canvas. Vienna, Austria. (Image source: Wikimedia Commons)

Page 184 (top): Ring of gold with enamel in the collection of Hallwylska museet, Stockholm. (Image source: Wikimedia Commons)

Page 184 (left): Lawrence, Sir Thomas. Portrait of the Honorable Mrs. Seymour Bathurst. 1828. Oil on canvas. Dallas Museum of Art, Dallas, Texas. (Image source: Wikimedia Commons)

Page 185 (top left): Lalique, René. Pansy Brooch. ca. 1903. Gold, glass, plique-à-jour enamel, sapphire. The Walters Art Museum, Baltimore. (Image source: The Walters Art Museum Online Collection)

Page 185 (top right): Pansy—Thoughtfulness, from the series Floral Beauties and Language of Flowers (N75) for Duke brand cigarettes. 1892. The Metropolitan Museum of Art. (Image source: Open Access at the Met)

Page 185 (bottom left): Plank, Josef. Bildnis Anna Reitter (geb. Lorenz). 1858. Oil on canvas. (Image source: Wikimedia Commons)

Page 185 (bottom right): Brooch in the form of a Pansy Brooch, ca. 1900. Cast gold, fired enamel, cut diamonds. Cooper Hewitt, Smithsonian Design Museum, New York. (Image source: Smithsonian Open Access)

Peacock

Page 186: Jeweled Collar in the Shape of a Peacock Feather. 1900. 18-carat gold, enamel, diamonds. Smithsonian American Art Museum, Washington, D.C. (Image source: Smithsonian Open Access)

Page 188 (left): Brooch in the Form of a Peacock. 2nd–3rd century CE. Champlevé enamel, bronze, garnet cabochon. The Metropolitan Museum of Art, New York. (Image source: Open Access at the Met)

Page 188 (right): Peacock Feather Brooch. Last quarter of the 19th century. Silver, diamonds, rubies, emeralds, gold. The Metropolitan Museum of Art, New York. (Image source: Open Access at the Met)

Page 189 (top left): Peacock and Dragon. 1878. Jacquard woven wool. Art Institute of Chicago, Chicago. (Image source: Art Institute of Chicago: Archival Collections)

Page 189 (right): Logsdail, William. Mary Leiter, Lady Curzon of Kedleston, wearing a 1903 gown by Jean-Philippe Worth. 1909. Oil on canvas. Kedleston Hall (National Trust), Derbyshire, UK. (Image source: Wikimedia Commons)

Page 189 (bottom): Frankish Peacock-Shaped Fibula. 5th–6th century CE. Gold, enamel. The Walters Art Museum, Baltimore. (Image source: The Walters Art Museum Online Collection)

Pearl

Page 190: Luttichuys, Isaack. Portrait of a Young Woman, Possibly Susanna Reael. 1656. Oil on canvas. (Image source: Rijksmuseum, Amsterdam)

Page 192 (top): Earrings. 6th–7th century. Gold, pearls. The Metropolitan Museum of Art, New York. (Image source: Open Access at the Met)

Page 192 (right): Mrs. John F. Kennedy Jr., White House, Mansion, Nursery. 1960s. Gelatin silver print. National Archives and Records Administration, Washington, D.C. (Image source: Wikimedia Commons)

Page 192 (bottom): Flameng, François. Zinaida Yusupova by Flameng (1894). 1894. Oil on panel. The State Hermitage Museum, St. Petersburg. (Image source: Wikimedia Commons)

Page 193 (top): Mummy Portrait: Woman with Necklace. ca. 161–192 CE. Encaustic on wood. Museum of Fine Arts, Boston. (Image source: Wikimedia Commons)

Page 193 (middle): Head of Venus. ca. 100 CE. Bronze with gold and pearl. The J. Paul Getty Museum, Los Angeles. (Image source: Getty's Special Collections and Institutional Archives)

Page 193 (bottom): Stieler, Joseph Karl. Crescentia Bourgin, 1833. Oil on canvas. Nymphenburg Palace. (Image source: Wikimedia Commons)

Peridot

Page 194: Ring with Peridot (Olivine). 17th century. Royal Armoury, Stockholm, Sweden. (Image source: Wikimedia Commons)

Page 196 (left): Intaglio with the head of Cleopatra II. ca. 175–115 BC. Peridot. The Walters Art Museum, Baltimore. (Image source: The Walters Art Museum Online Collection)

Page 196 (right): Marcus and Co. Brooch. ca. 1900. Gold, peridot, diamonds, pearls, and enamel. The Metropolitan Museum of Art, New York. (Image source: Open Access at the Met)

Page 197 (left): Largillierre, Nicolas de. Portrait de la comédienne Marie-Anne de Châteauneuf, dite Mlle Duclos (1664–1747), dans le rôle d'Ariane. 1710s. Oil on Canvas. Musée du Louvre, Paris. (Image source: Wikimedia Commons)

Page 197 (right): Antique Suffragette Amethyst and Peridot Pendant. 1905. (Image source: Bell and Bird, Austin)

Page 197 (bottom): Brooch with Peridot. ca. 1908–11. Gold, brown, and white enamel brooch with a peridot olivine. (Image source: Rijksmuseum, Amsterdam)

Ruby

Page 198: Raja Ravi Varma. Rani Bharani Thirunal Lakshmi Bayi of Travancore. 1883. Sree Chitra Art Gallery, Thiruvananthapuram, India. (Image source: Wikimedia Commons)

Page 200 (right): Pair of Earrings (part of a set). 18th century. The Metropolitan Museum of Art, New York. (Image source: Open Access at the Met)

Page 200 (bottom): Gheeraerts, Marcus (the Younger). Portrait of Margaret Layton (formerly Laton). ca. 1620. The Victoria and Albert Museum, London, United Kingdom. (Image source: Wikimedia Commons)

Page 201 (top left): Renaldi, Francesco. Portrait of a Mughal Woman. 1787. The Metropolitan Museum of Art, New York. (Image source: Open Access at the Met)

Page 201 (top right): Gold Ring with a Pink Sapphire and Diamonds. (Image source: Inez Stodel, Amsterdam)

Page 201 (bottom right): Crivelli, Carlo. Madonna and Child. ca. 1480. The Metropolitan Museum of Art, New York. (Image source: Open Access at the Met)

Scarab

Page 202: Egyptian. Heart Scarab of Hatnefer. ca. 1492–1473 BCE. The Metropolitan Museum of Art, New York. (Image source: Open Access at the Met)

Page 204 (top): Melillo, Giacinto. Egyptian-Style Necklace with Scarabs. Late 19th–early 20th century. The Walters Art Museum, Baltimore. (Image source: The Walters Art Museum Online Collection)

Page 204 (bottom): Long, Edwin Longsden. A Votary of Isis. 1883. (Image source: Wikimedia Commons)

Page 205 (top): Egyptian. Mummy Mask of a Woman. ca. 1st century CE. The Walters Art Museum, Baltimore. (Image source: The Walters Art Museum Online Collection)

Page 205 (bottom): Scarab with Wings. Egyptian. 1070–525 BCE (Third Intermediate–early Late Period). Faience with blue glaze. The Walters Art Museum, Baltimore. (Image source: The Walters Art Museum Online Collection)

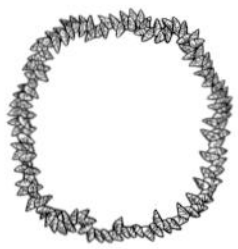

Shell

Page 206: Jensen, Christian Albrecht. Cathrine Jensen, née Lorenzen, the Artist's Wife Wearing a Turban. 1842–1844. Statens Museum for Kunst, Copenhagen. (Image source: Wikimedia Commons)

Page 208 (left): Dicksee, Thomas Francis. Miranda. c. 1895. Oil on canvas. Private collection. (Image source: Wikimedia Commons)

Page 208 (right): "Shell beads and ornaments from Paquimé (Casas Grandes culture)." c. 1150–1350 CE. Trade/ornamental object from the Paquimé region. Arizona State Museum. (Image source: Arizona State Museum, Library and Archives)

Page 209 (top left): Egyptian string of beads with 19 small speckled pierced univalve shells, before 3850 B.C. Harvard University—Boston Museum of Fine Arts Expedition (Image source: Open Image Collection at MFA Boston)

Page 209 (right): Lotto, Lorenzo. Portrait of Lucina Brembati. 1521–1523. Accademia Carrara, Bergamo. (Image source: Wikimedia Commons)

Page 209 (bottom): Sandys, Emma. A Young Female Musician. 1864. Oil on panel. (Norwich, England.) (Image source: Wikimedia Commons)

Snakes

Page 210: Merle, Georges. L'Envoûteuse (The Sorceress). 1883. Birmingham Museum of Art, Birmingham, AL. (Image source: The Birmingham Museum of Art Archives)

Page 212 (left): Gold Snake Ring. Roman, 1st century CE. The Metropolitan Museum of Art, New York. (Image source: Open Access at the Met)

Page 212 (right): Mummy Mask of a Woman. Roman Period (A.D. 60–70). The Metropolitan Museum of Art, New York. (Image source: Open Access at the Met)

Page 213 (top): Yakovlev, Gavriil. Portrait of Julia Telyakovskaya. 1848. Hermitage Museum, Saint Petersburg. (Image source: Wikimedia Commons)

Page 213 (middle right): Brooch in the Form of a Snake with Sapphire. ca. 1870–1890. Rijksmuseum, Amsterdam. (Image source: Wikimedia Commons)

Page 213 (bottom left): Vintage 1910s paste snake brooch. (Image source: Erie Basin, New York)

Page 213 (bottom right): Vernon, Émile. Fille au citronnier. 1913. Private collection. (Image source: Wikimedia Commons)

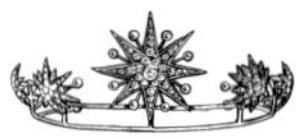

Stars

Page 214: Winterhalter, Franz Xaver. Portrait of Sophia Frederika Mathilda (1818–77), Princess of Württemberg. 1863–73. (Image source: Rijksmuseum, Amsterdam)

Page 216 (top): Winterhalter, Franz Xaver. Victoria, Princess Royal. 1867 Buckingham Palace, London. (Image source: The Royal Archives)

Page 216 (left): Jewelry Element in the Shape of a Star. ca. 1390–1353 BCE. The Metropolitan Museum of Art, New York. (Image source: Open Access at the Met)

Page 216 (bottom right): First Lady Jacqueline Kennedy Attends a Dinner for Minister of State for Cultural Affairs of France, André Malraux. 1962. North Portico, White House, Washington, D.C. (Image source: Wikimedia Commons)

Page 217 (top left): Paste Star Brooch. ca.

1840. Silver set with foil–backed paste (lead–crystal) stones. (Image source: Erie Basin, New York)

Page 217 (top right): Winterhalter, Franz Xaver. Elisabeth of Austria. 1865. Kunsthistorisches Museum, Vienna Austria. (Image source: Wikimedia Commons)

Page 217 (bottom left): Leffler, Warren K. Jacqueline Kennedy at the White House. 11 April 1962. (Image source: Wikimedia Commons)

Page 217 (bottom right): EB Modern Shooting Star ring. (Image source: Erie Basin, New York)

Sun

Page 218: French Pilgrim's Badge with Sun with human face, fifteenth century. Lead. Metropolitan Museum of Art, New York. (Image source: Open Access at the Met)

Page 220 (left): Anonymous. Paper lantern, ca 1880. Metropolitan Museum, New York. (Image source: Open Access at the Met)

Page 220 (right): Cartier Mythological Sun Seal Ring, circa 1960. (Image source: Inez Stodel, Amsterdam)

Page 221 (top): Gasser, Leonardo. Portrait of a Young Italian woman, nineteenth century. Private collection (Image source: Wikimedia Commons)

Page 221 (bottom left): Merle, Hugues. The Neapolitan Girl, 1876. Private collection. (Image source: Wikimedia Commons)

Page 221 (bottom right): 1980s Vintage Sun Brooch. (Image source: Erie Basin)

Swallow

Page 222: Swallow Amulet. ca. 664–380 B.C. Egypt. The Metropolitan Museum of Art, New York. (Image source: Open Access at the Met)

Page 224 (top): Victorian Swallow Brooch. 1890s. 14K Yellow Gold, Seed Pearls, and 0.07ct Old European Cut Diamond. (Image source: Erie Basin, New York)

Page 224 (middle): Swallow Brooch. ca. 1900. 14K gold and enamel with cushion-cut diamond. American maker. (Image source: Inez Stodel, Amsterdam)

Page 224 (bottom): Swallow earrings. C1890. Silver, 14K, rose cute diamonds and rubies. (Image source: Erie Basin, New York)

Page 225: Van der Helst, Bartholomeus. Portrait of a Young Girl in a Pale Blue Dress with an Ostrich-Feather Fan. 1645. National Gallery, London. (Image source: Wikimedia Commons)

Swan

Page 226: Barney, Alice Pike. Kate Deering Ridgely. After 1900. Smithsonian American Art Museum, Washington, D.C. (Image source: Smithsonian Open Access)

Page 228 (left): Mata Hari, 1910. [Photograph] (Image source: Wikimedia Commons)

Page 228 (right): A Swan. ca. 1270. Illuminated Manuscript. The J. Paul Getty Museum, Los Angeles. (Image source: Getty's Special Collections and Institutional Archives)

Page 229 (top left): Pickenoy, Nicolaes Eliasz. Portrait of a Young Woman. 1632. The J. Paul Getty Museum, Los Angeles. (Image source: Getty's Special Collections and Institutional Archives)

Page 229 (top right): Chelsea Porcelain Manufactory. Seal. ca. 1751–54. The Metropolitan Museum of Art, New York (Image source: Open Access at the Met)

Page 229 (bottom): The Dunstable Swan Jewel. ca. 1400. British Museum, London. (Image source: Wikimedia Commons)

Tassel

Page 230: Varma, Raja Ravi. Thara Varini. 1896. Collection of Dr. M. A. Chidambaram, Chennai. (Image source: Wikimedia Commons)

Page 232 (left): Ingres, Jean-Auguste-Dominique. Madame Moitessier. 1851. Oil on canvas. National Gallery of Art, Washington, D.C. (Image source: Wikimedia Commons)

Page 232 (right): Hairnet. 225–175 B.C. Greek; made in Egypt. Gold, garnet, and glass paste. The J. Paul Getty Museum, Los Angeles. (Image source: Getty's Special Collections and Institutional Archives)

Page 233 (top): Gold Eye-Shaped Pendant with Three Tassels. 6th–5th century B.C. Cypriot. Gold and silver. The Metropolitan Museum of Art, New York. (Image source: Open Access at the Met)

Page 233 (left): Castellani, Firm of. Necklace with Cameo of Veronica's Veil. ca. 1870. The Metropolitan Museum of Art, New York. (Image source: Open Access at the Met)

Page 233 (bottom): Haudebourt-Lescot, Hortense. Portrait of a Lady in a Wooded Landscape. ca. 1830. Private collection. (Image source: Wikimedia Commons)

Topaz

Page 234: Earrings (France). Early 19th century. Topaz, silver, and gold. Cooper Hewitt, Smithsonian Design Museum, New York. (Image source: Smithsonian Open Access)

Page 236 (top): Necklace. Probably French. Late 16th century. Metropolitan Museum of Art. (Image source: Open Access at the Met)

Page 236 (bottom): Hair Accessory. ca. 1830. French silver gilt with topaz. The Metropolitan Museum of Art, New York. (Image source: Open Access at the Met)

Page 237 (top): Kruseman, Jan Adam. Portrait of Alida Christina Assink. 1833. (Image source: Rijksmuseum, Amsterdam)

Page 237 (left): Earrings (France). 19th century. Gold, silver, topaz, and pearls. Cooper Hewitt, Smithsonian Design Museum, New York. (Image source: Smithsonian Open Access)

Page 237 (bottom right): Dürck, Friedrich. Bildnis der Caroline Krafft (geb. Platner). 1835. Munich, Germany. (Image source: Wikimedia Commons)

Turquoise

Page 238: Winterhalter, Franz Xaver. The Linked Hands of Queen Victoria (1819–1901) and Prince Albert (1819–1861). ca. 1840–1860. Royal Collection Trust, United Kingdom. (Image source: Wikimedia Commons)

Page 240 (left): Eagle, Annie. Squash Blossom Necklace by Annie Eagle. Silver and turquoise. Contemporary. (Image source: Wikimedia Commons)

Page 240 (right): Burbank, Elbridge Ayer. Estzan-Nap-Pa. 1910. Oil on canvas. Smithsonian American Art Museum, Washington, D.C. (Image source: Smithsonian Open Access)

Page 241 (top): Sandys, Frederick (Anthony Frederick Augustus). Grace Rose. 1866. Yale Center for British Art, New Haven. (Image source: Yale Center for British Art)

Page 241 (bottom): Bracelet. 11th–12th century. Attributed to Syria. Gold and turquoise. The Metropolitan Museum of Art, New York. (Image source: Open Access at the Met)

Violet

Page 242: Girodet-Trioson, Anne Louis. Madame Jacques-Louis-Étienne Reizet (Colette-Désirée-Thérèse Godefroy, 1782–1850). 1823. Oil on canvas. The Metropolitan Museum of Art, New York. (Image source: Open Access at the Met)

Page 244 (top): Hanger met viooltje (Pendant with Violet). ca. 1930–1940. Dutch Indies. Gold filigree. Rijksmuseum, Amsterdam. (Image source: Wikimedia Commons)

Page 244 (bottom): Harlequin violet ring, 1790. (Image source: Inez Stodel, Amsterdam)

Page 245 (top): Winterhalter, Franz Xaver. Portrait of Elizabeth Ivanovna Suvorova (née Basilevskaya). 1860. (Image source: Wikimedia Commons)

Page 245 (bottom left): Sandys, Emma. Rosabelle. 1865. (Panel.) (Image source: Art History Project)

Page 245 (bottom right): Branch Brooch. ca. 1945–1953. The Hague. Gold, chalcedony, ruby, pearl, and diamond. (Image source: Rijksmuseum, Amsterdam)

Wheat

Page 246: Tiffany & Co., Wheat Diamond Brooch. Gold and diamonds. Museum of Fine Arts, Boston. (Image source: MFA Images)

Page 248 (top): Brooch (France). ca. 1800. Gold, silver, and diamonds. Cooper Hewitt, Smithsonian Design Museum, New York. (Image source: Smithsonian Open Access)

Page 248 (bottom): Ingres, Jean-Auguste-Dominique. Madame Jacques-Louis Leblanc. 1823. Oil on canvas. The Metropolitan Museum of Art, New York. (Image source: Open Access at the Met)

Page 249 (top): Westin, Fredric. Desideria, 1781–1860, Queen of Sweden and Norway, Wife of Karl XIV Johan. 1830. Oil on canvas. National Portrait Gallery of Sweden, Nationalmuseum, Stockholm.

Page 249 (bottom left): English wheatsheaf earrings. (Image source: Bell and Bird, Austin)

Page 249 (bottom right): Schmiechen, Hermann. Princess Mary Adelaide, Duchess of Teck (1833–97). 1882. Royal Collection Trust, UK. (Image source: Wikimedia Commons)

Wreath

Page 250: Kameo: Tiberius. Roman, Caesar Tiberius (r. 14–37 CE). Diorite cameo. Kunsthistorisches Museum, Vienna. (Image source: Wikimedia Commons)

Page 252 (top): Golden Laurel Wreath. Hellenistic era. Gold. Kerameikos Archaeological Museum, Athens. (Image source: Wikimedia Commons)

Page 252 (bottom): Lalique, René. Laurel Leaves Brooch. ca. 1903. Pink pearl, mother-of-pearl, enamel, and gold. The Walters Art Museum, Baltimore. (Image source: The Walters Art Museum Online Collection)

Page 253 (top): Comerre, Léon François. A Classical Beauty. ca. 1890. Oil on canvas. Private collection. (Image source: Wikimedia Commons)

Page 253 (middle): Gérard, François. Napoleon in Coronation Robes. 1806. Oil on canvas. French State Collection. (Image source: Wikimedia Commons)

Page 253 (bottom): Wreath Consisting of Laurel and Oak Branches. ca. 1760–70. French. Gilt bronze. The Metropolitan Museum of Art, New York. (Image source: Open Access at the Met)

EMERALD DOUBLE RING, 1895.

Page 270 (top): Marcus and Co. Jewelers, 1895. Double ring. Metropolitan Museum of Art. (Image source: Open Access at the Met)

Page 270 (bottom): Garnet heart brooch, ca. 1770. Metropolitan Museum of Art. (Image source: Open Access at the Met)

Page 271 (top right): Snake bracelet, Roman, 1st century AD. Metropolitan Museum of Art. (Image source: Open Access at the Met)

Page 271 (left): Spencer, Lilly Martin. *We Both Must Fade (Mrs. Fithian)*, 1869. Oil on canvas. Smithsonian American Art Museum. (Image source: Smithsonian Open Access)

Page 271 (bottom right): Pair of gold earrings with an Egyptian Atef crown set with stones and glass. 3rd–2nd century BC. Metropolitan Museum of Art. (Image source: Open Access at the Met)

EIGHTEENTH CENTURY HEART BROOCH SET WITH GARNETS.

ROMAN SNAKE BRACELET.

JEWELRY BOX, 1869.

ANCIENT GREEK EARRINGS.

Clarkson Potter/Publishers
An imprint of the Crown Publishing Group
A division of Penguin Random House LLC
1745 Broadway
New York, NY 10019
clarksonpotter.com
penguinrandomhouse.com

Photo credits are located on pp. 258-270.
Front cover photographs: (top right) Erie Basin, New York; (left) Open Access at the Met; (middle right) Open Access at the Met; (bottom left) Rijksmuseum, Amsterdam; (bottom right) Erie Basin, New York
Back cover photographs: (top left) Open Access at the Met; (top right) MFA Images; (middle right) Open Access at the Met; (bottom left) MFA Images; (bottom right) Smithsonian Open Access

Library of Congress Cataloging-in-Publication Data
Names: Azzarito, Amy author
Title: Secret language of victorian jewelry : The history and lore of gems, charms, and talismans / Amy Azzarito.
Description: First edition. | New York : Clarkson Potter/Publishers, [2026]
Identifiers: LCCN 2025044087 | ISBN 9798217034833 hardcover | ISBN 9798217034840 ebook
Subjects: LCSH: Jewelry, Victorian—Miscellanea | Clothing and dress—Symbolic aspects
Classification: LCC NK7109.85.V53 A99 2026 | DDC 739.27—dc23/eng/20251210
LC record available at https://lccn.loc.gov/2025044087

ISBN 979-8-217-03483-3
Ebook ISBN 979-8-217-03484-0

Editor: Emma Brodie
Assistant Editor: Briana James
Designer: Ian Dingman
Production designer: Christina Self
Production editor: Isabella Franco
Production: Jesssica Heim
Compositor: Merri Ann Morrell
Copy editor: Alison Kerr Miller
Proofreaders: Rita Madrigal and Robin Slutzky
Marketer: Chloe Aryeh

Manufactured in China

10 9 8 7 6 5 4 3 2 1

First Edition

The authorized representative in the EU for product safety and compliance is Penguin Random House Ireland, Morrison Chambers, 32 Nassau Street, Dublin D02 YH68, Ireland, https://eu-contact.penguin.ie.

Amy Azzarito is a design historian, author, and journalist whose work uncovers the histories woven into everyday objects. She is the author of *Past & Present* (Abrams, 2013) and *The Elements of a Home* (Chronicle Books, 2020). She is currently completing her PhD dissertation on the role of women jewelers in eighteenth-century Britain at the University of York, UK. Amy lives in Marin County, California, with her daughter, Stella; husband, Mark; and cat, Freya.